THE DUST NEVER SETTLES

The incredible story of a female police
officer's 23 days at Ground Zero

STACEY GOODMAN

ISBN: 9798542600871

DEDICATION

To Danny, my brother, my friend. He always watched out for me when I was young. He included me in family events, despite our differences. He always welcomed me.

I wanted to share this with you, though you were taken from us far too soon.

Love you, miss you.

————————

CONTENTS

Chapter 1 — Into Hell...17

Chapter 2 — The Sounds of Silence.................28

Chapter 3 — Headquarters.............................42

Chapter 4 — Take My Breath Away.................48

Chapter 5 — First Hero..................................57

Chapter 6 — Bone of My Bones.....................70

Chapter 7 — Life and Death...........................86

Chapter 8 — In Our Genes.............................98

Chapter 9 — We All Saw................................109

Chapter 10 — Activated.................................123

Chapter 11 — 23 Nights on the Pile...............143

Chapter 12 — Brothers In Arms.....................155

Chapter 13 — Detective Goodman.................165

Chapter 14 — A Brief Lapse of Judgment.......178

Chapter 15 — Aftermath................................191

Chapter 16 — I Will Always Remember You.....197

Afterword..215

ACKNOWLEDGMENTS

All the hard-working and dedicated people I worked with
day in and day out on the Pile.
Those I worked with at one time, or tirelessly every night.
The heroes that have left us, and those who still remain.
Police, Fire, steel and iron workers, utility workers,
construction workers, and government employees.

I would especially like to thank all the men and women of the
Suffolk County Police Department, with whom I have had the
distinct honor and privilege of working side-by-side, and
getting to know. Their tireless dedication to the communities
and citizens of Suffolk County, Long Island, New York,
serving day in and day out, going above and beyond the call
of duty.

I want to thank my friends, the ones who stayed, the ones
that did not judge decisions I made or differences of opinion
we had. To the friends who keep in touch, even though it
seems I am half a world away.
My new friends; may our best days lie head.

James, who made this book possible.

———————

Chapter 1 — Into Hell

I sat anxiously in the darkened van, my federal khaki uniform stiff and clean, looking ahead nervously with the others on my team. We were the only vehicle in the oddly dark Battery Tunnel as far as I could tell, but my focus was straight ahead at the murky void that awaited us at the top of the incline. I'd come into the city through the tunnel dozens of times, but never with such trepidation at what awaited us just a minute ahead. The old, white unmarked federal van climbed and shined its headlights forward trying to illuminate the murky hollow that lay at the end of the shaft. It gave me an eerie feeling, like being inside a long serpent, about to be expelled through its mouth into the battle-weary night. For another minute we strained our eyes to see beyond the portal to the hell that lay just beyond. As we rose and approached the exit, the world just outside began to take on a ghastly, horrific form.

The first thing I could make out was roiling clouds of dust and smoke, brightly backlit by high-powered emergency spotlights. It looked like a movie set to me. A movie about post-apocalyptic devastation in a third-world country. The dust churned up everywhere in the air as if a great machine hovered, voraciously consuming the city from above. As we approached the mouth of the tunnel everything my brain normally anticipated as I emerged was missing. It was a gargantuan, gaping landscape that looked more like a lunar bombing accident than the financial center of the entire world.

* * *

I was six years old and my mother looked me straight in the eye and said, "Where the fuck did you learn to talk like that?!"

It didn't take a Suffolk County Police Detective to figure that one out.

I was a streetwise little girl, even at five or six years old, and would often walk the one block to the nearby strip of stores, a supermarket and a bank. As I turned the corner from my house as I had done many times before, a middle-aged man pulled up in a big white shitty car and opened the passenger door. I can still remember the look of the metallic gold vinyl bench seat and the stench of cigarette smoke. He asked me to help him find his lost puppy. "Take a fucking hike, ass hole," was my standard response—which drew a quick look of shock, then the would-be child molester hit the gas and got as far away from me as he could. It happened more than you'd like to believe. I hate to think about all of the innocent little girls who fell for that bullshit.

When I was nine, my mother was dating a man named Jack. He was round-faced, wore glasses and had patchy red hair that was combed over. A real prize. Mother brought Jack around a lot, and he stayed overnight quite often. He always gave me a creepy vibe and I avoided him as much as possible.

My room was in the back of our single-story, east coast ranch style house. It was adjacent to my mother's room and I would be horrified by the noises I would hear coming through the paper-thin walls when Jack stayed over. One night, a couple of hours after I'd been traumatized by their raucous activities, I was lying in my bed trying to fall asleep. I heard a noise that sounded like my mother's door opening. I opened my eyes and listened carefully. I heard quiet footsteps coming toward my room. I lay motionless as I heard my door open. I closed my eyes because I didn't want to get into trouble for being awake so late. After a minute I squinted enough to see it was Jack, bare ass naked standing next to my bed. I closed my eyes tight, hoping he would just go away. But he didn't.

I suddenly felt something fleshy on my mouth. What the fucking hell?! I thought I would give it a second chance for a peaceful resolution, so I pretended to be asleep, and rolled over turning away from him. I heard a faint noise coming from my mother's room and Jack rushed out of my room and disappeared into the darkness.

As street wise and tough as I was, I was traumatized by Jack's sexual assault. I started having nightmares about it, and developed trouble sleeping. I didn't tell my mother, or anyone what he had done. I guess I figured that she wouldn't believe me, and would just take his side. That seemed even worse than not telling.

A few years later my mother was dating a different man and mentioned that she wanted him to move in. "No fucking way," I told her. "You know that ass hole Jack—he fucking snuck into my room one night and tried to put his dick into my mouth when I was only nine."

"You're just making that up," she shot back.

* * *

I have a twin brother, a much older half-sister and a half-brother, Danny. We had our mother in common, but different fathers. My mother had serious mental issues, which made our lives extremely difficult when she was around, and when she would go missing for days or weeks at a time. She suffered from what the doctors called manic depression, which is now labeled bipolar depression. Bipolar depression is character-ized, clinicians tell us, by periods of depression followed by periods of psychosis or mania (Please keep hands, arms, legs, and feet inside at all times, because we're taking off for a fucking roller-coaster ride), which is elevated mood swings and can cause a person to make poor decisions without regard for the consequences, and become quite irritable, among other side effects. Oh, yeah. At the time, bipolar depression was treated with high doses of lithium, which my mother would take only 'when she felt like it,' causing even more problems—mostly for me, not her.

My mother's parents, my grandparents, were very good grandparents. They were everything my mother was not—stable, reliable, caring and nurturing. My grandfather was a successful businessman, and I learned later that the only reason we'd enjoyed a steady roof over our heads during my childhood on Long Island was because he had purchased the house and took care of the mortgage payments. My twin brother and I had been a "surprise" in my mother's life, and she had us at 40, so her parents did their part to ease our burden by providing us with a home in a quiet suburban neighborhood.

Although my mother had received a good education and had a steady job working for the state of New York, she was terrible with money and would often run out at critical times. If not for the financial support of my grandparents, we surely would have ended up on the streets.

My grandparents were born in the old country, Eastern European, and brought their work ethic and gratitude for America's many opportunities with them. I liked my grandparents, and respected them—but in retrospect, I underappreciated them. Mother would dump us on them on weekends and I would hang out in their Bronx apartment with them. What I really liked was my grandmother's cooking. Everything my mother cooked was first poured out of a can. My grandmother, however, was an excellent cook, and the apartment was always filled with wonderful smells when I was there.

My Grandfather was diagnosed with cancer, and back then it was a death sentence—they just sent you home to die. I went to see him one last time. I sat next to him and my grandmother was caring for him. I learned from her how to care for others. It was my first experience with death and dying.

My mother was very smart, in her own way, and during the manic periods would interact with me at times. She taught me how to play games like Rummy, Scrabble and Backgammon. She was very good at them, and taught me well. Mother would take us into New York City when she was feeling well. When I was ten years old we went to the World Trade Center for the first time. We had heard about the high speed elevators and were excited to give them a try. We ran for the elevators once inside the newly opened towers and pushed the button to go as high as we could. We were amazed how fast it was.

As a child I felt like a rocket taking off, and within mere seconds we would be at 110 stories. Then we would push the lobby button and descend so quickly it felt like a rollercoaster going straight down; your stomach would feel like it was in your mouth and your feet would be lifting off the floor. Back then there was no security, and my mother thought it was a good idea to leave us playing there while she went about her business.

The house we lived in was constantly disheveled and in disrepair (I wrote that she let it go to shit, but others suggested these more pleasant descriptive terms). Mother would be there at times, and gone at other times—as I said, sometimes for days or weeks at a time. Although I was very young, it was somehow up to me to feed myself and take care of the house while she was God knows where. I would go to the store with what little money I had, whatever I was able to squirrel away, and buy Chef Boyardee canned pasta, because that's all I knew how to heat up. As a child I went to bed hungry many nights.

When I was older, I was fortunate enough to make friends with the girl who lived around the corner from me. She was kind and sweet and had a lovely family; the total opposite of me and my existence. Her mother was a wonderful, large Italian woman who knew how to cook, and was very happy to feed me. I was so appreciative of this oasis of love and care.

When my older brother Danny still lived with us, he would do his best to take care of us, but he was just a young adult himself and it wasn't fair for him to have that kind of responsibility dumped on his shoulders. He did become a father later in life, and was a wonderful father, and raised four successful children.

As I got older, Mother would sometimes leave a little money on the counter when she planned to disappear. If I found money on the countertop I knew she would not be home and the money was to be used for food. I would clean up the house and straighten things up. But she would only see it as an insult to her 'lady of the house' efforts and get upset with me for throwing it in her face. Yes, I was around seven or eight when this shit was going down.

I do not write or say these things lightly or to make anyone feel sorry for me, but to put into perspective how I learned to survive at a very young age, and how I came to be who I am today.

Because I grew up poor I had always promised myself I would work and never have to rely on anyone for money. I would hustle any way I could before I was old enough to get a job. I would stand outside the grocery store and ask people if I could carry their bags to their car. When I was older I got a paper route. My grandfather taught me the value of money. He would sit me down and show me how to save money, and if I saved enough I could spend a little without feeling guilty, he would say. He demonstrated this by putting a $10 bill in front of me and telling me I should put that $10 in the bank—to a child back then, that was a lot of money. Then my grandfather handed me a $1 bill and told me I could spend it anyway I wanted. I got it. The ten went in the bank, and the one went to the store.

It wasn't always bleak. Some happier times came when my half-sister was living in Vermont. I would spend a month in the summer with her at her quaint townhouse nestled in the woods on the outskirts of civilization, surrounded by wildlife and nature. My sister and her neighbors had a beautiful garden, with lettuce and assorted vegetables. One summer she sent me to a horse riding camp where I learned how to take care of, groom, and ride the horses. To this day I still find joy in horseback riding.

I was very close to my half-brother, Danny, and was sad to lose him to cancer. He was the one in the family who reached out to me the most and took an interest in my life, and made sure I was included in family activities. After a member of Danny's family, no blood relation to me, perished in the towers on 9/11, I was given special leave to attend the memorial service that was held in Connecticut. Danny was speaking during the service and suddenly stopped speaking about the deceased, and instead wanted to recognize me. Danny told everyone how I was working at Ground Zero every day and helping the victims, and that I had to receive special permission to be in attendance that day. Danny asked me to stand and be recognized by everyone.

Normally, I would have been happy to be recognized, but this was different. I shifted uncomfortably in my seat and slowly stood as I held back tears. Most of what I did in my career under the heading of "serve and protect" went essentially unnoticed by the members of my family and by the communities I served. But I felt a genuine sense of gratitude from those in attendance that day. I was always proud of Danny for many reasons. My brother was liberal politically, but had a capitalistic drive that made him a successful entrepreneur. He started a business essentially in his garage and built it on his own.

■ ■ ■

September 11, 2001 — 05:41

Mohamed Atta, a licensed commercial pilot, and his close associate, Abdulaziz al-Omari, Islamic extremists and members of al-Qaida, arrived at Portland International Jetport at Portland, Maine at 5:41 a.m. to catch the early flight to Boston. Atta walked up to the American Airlines ticket counter and asked ticket agent Mike Tuohey, "I need my boarding pass for Flight 11."

Tuohey looked at the computer screen and told Atta that he could only give him his boarding pass for the flight to Boston. "You'll have to check in a second time when you get to Logan."

Mohamed Atta clenched his jaw and his face reddened. He appeared to calm himself purposefully, then said, "I was told I have one-step check-in."

Ticket Agent Tuohey looked at him, then back at the computer. "You need to hurry if you don't want to miss your flight."

Atta glared at Tuohey for a moment and glanced up at the clock, then signaled to al-Omari, and they both left the ticket counter and headed for the security checkpoint, clutching their first-class tickets with a connecting flight from Boston to Los Angeles. The two terrorists boarded Flight 5930, which was scheduled to depart from Portland at 06:00.

The plane arrived on time in Boston at 06:45, the same time three other terrorists, Waleed al-Shehri, Wail al-Shehri, and Satam al-Suqami arrived. Seven minutes later, Marwan al-Shehhi, the hijacker pilot of United Airlines Flight 175, placed a call to Atta's cell phone, confirming everything was a 'go.'

Atta and al-Omari had to go through the check-in and security screening at Boston before they could board American Airlines Flight 11 for Los Angeles. Atta was pissed, but he controlled his anger and checked in and got his boarding pass, then went through security. Suqami, Wail al-Shehri, and Waleed al-Shehri got checked in as well.

The airliner had just come in from San Francisco and was being readied for the flight to Los Angeles, and copilot First Officer Lynn Howland walked off the jetway and into the passenger lounge and looked around. Mohamed Atta approached her and asked, "Will you be flying the plane back across the country?"

"No," she said. "I just brought it in from San Francisco."

Atta turned on his heels and walked away from her. As the Flight 11 began boarding, Atta stopped at the desk and asked a gate agent, "Do you know if the two bags I checked in on my flight from Portland have been loaded onto the plane?"

The agent looked at the computer, and said, "Sorry, it doesn't look like they made the plane in Portland." Atta frowned, then walked onto the jetway and boarded the plane.

The five hijackers were aboard Flight 11 just moments before its scheduled departure at 7:45 a.m. Atta sat in business class, seat 8D, and al-Omari was seated in 8G, with Suqami in 10B. Wail al-Shehri and Waleed were together in first class, in seats 2B and 2A.

American Airlines Flight 11 to Los Angeles carried 81 passengers and 11 crew members; about half its capacity. The crew members were Captain John Ogonowski and First Officer Thomas McGuinness Jr., a former Navy fighter pilot. The flight attendants were Barbara Arestegui, Jeffrey Collman, Sara Low, Karen Martin, Kathleen Nicosia, Betty Ong, Jean Roger, Dianne Snyder and Amy Sweeney. Some of the well-known passengers on the flight were the creator and executive producer of the television program "Frasier," David Angell, and his wife Lynn Angell. Also onboard was model and actress Berry Berenson, the widow of Anthony Perkins. "Family Guy" creator Seth MacFarlane, arrived too late and missed the flight, and actor Mark Wahlberg changed his ticket at the last minute.

As the crew readied the airliner for takeoff, flight service manager Michael Woodward walked onto the plane for his final check, looking around and noticing passenger Mohamed Atta glaring at him, and locking eyes with him momentarily. He didn't like the look Atta gave him, but because they were up against the schedule, he took a last look around, then walked back to the door and stepped through to the jetway. The pilot received clearance from the tower, and they pushed back from the gate and headed for the runway. The aircraft began to pick up speed, and lifted its wheels from the Logan International Airport runway at 7:59 a.m.

Around fifteen minutes into the flight the pilots turned off the "Fasten Seatbelt" signs, and the five hijackers took that as their cue to begin. They immediately stabbed flight attendants Karen Martin and Barbara Arestegui and slashed the throat of passenger Daniel Lewin, an American-Israeli Internet entrepreneur who understood Arabic, and had served as an officer in the elite Sayeret Matkal Special Operations Unit of the Israel Defense Forces. They then fought their way into the cockpit and killed the pilot and copilot. Mohamed Atta took the controls and turned the plane toward Manhattan.

Flight attendant Betty Ong made it to the American Airlines emergency line and told them, "Okay, my name is Betty Ong. I'm Number 3 on Flight 11. Our Number 1 got stabbed. Our purser is stabbed. Nobody knows who stabbed who and we can't even get up to business class right now because nobody can breathe. And we can't get to the cockpit, the door won't open."

Those on the ground kept attempting to contact Flight 11 but no response came, and someone in the cockpit turned off the flight's Mode-C transponder signal.

Chapter 2 — The Sounds of Silence

Those who designed the Battery Park Tunnel brought you up out of the river and you would see Battery Park and the majestic Twin Towers right in front of you, welcoming you to lower Manhattan. It was beautifully designed, and a gorgeous sight as you exited the tunnel—but not on this night. As we drove through the empty tunnel we finally came out and saw nothing but a desolate landscape—roiling smoke and dust pierced through from behind by shocking bright lights. Everything was jagged rubble covered in the thick layer of dust with jutting debris as far as you could see. I looked up at the scene, and although I knew what was happening, my brain couldn't process what I was seeing. My most coherent thought was that I was arriving on a movie set in a scene from a distant, inhospitable planet.

Our plain white government van picked its way around piles of ash-covered debris as we entered Ground Zero for the first time. We looked through the thin protective barrier the dark tinted windows provided, and surveyed our surroundings in disbelief. The van rolled to a stop and someone in an ash gray covered uniform opened the door. We looked at one another, then began to crawl through the opening in the side of the van, emerging in a foreign, bizarre world. My eyes were scanning the panorama, looking for anything recognizable. I knew this place well—I had been coming here since I was a child—but there was nothing identifiable within my view. I was in shock. I didn't know what I was looking at. My brain was having trouble processing what my eyes were seeing. Piles of rubble with twisted steel beams at least ten stories high threatened to shift and fall throughout the scene. Churning plumes of smoke and ash bubbled up into the surrounding buildings, creating a smokey snow globe effect around us.

My ears were just as confused. I had been here many times before, and my brain thought it knew something about this place. But there was nothing even remotely earthly about it. There weren't even any normal sounds. I stopped and listened for a moment, and realized that not only were the familiar noises of traffic and voices absent, but there was no sign of life in the air whatsoever. It was a dead zone. There were no birds. No traffic lights. No trees. There was no sound. What little noise that was created by our feet, or a moving vehicle, or a working machine across the Pile was absorbed by the thick dust, muting the normal reflections of noise as if we were in the center of a gigantic soundproof booth. 'Dead sound.' The thought of fresh snow came to mind as I looked around and listened—the way it covers everything and mutes the sound. But snow was beautiful, and this—this was a waking nightmare.

No one spoke. We all stood in silent reverence—on what we knew would be hallowed ground. The tip of one of my steel-toed boots moved some of the gray powder, and a small cloud swirled near the ground. Everywhere there was movement around the Pile, there was a cloud of ash swirling. *I don't want to be breathing that shit*, I thought.

People in obvious authority approached our van and I saw they were dressed in the same beige khaki uniform as mine. A man spoke to us for a few minutes, then he motioned for us to follow him. I could see through the backdrop of the bright lights, the unique tubular skeletal structure that revealed the site of the towers. Now, it looked like something out of a horror movie. The base of the structure was protruding from the rubble with bright light shining through, giving the appearance of a skeleton reaching up from the grave.

Ground Zero was entirely covered in thick gray dust. The two Towers had collapsed and in the process had pulverized everything within them. Of the thousands of pieces of furniture that filled over 200 floors of office space, I didn't see a single piece of furniture in the rubble. Besides twisted metal and broken chunks of concrete, the only thing that I saw that was intact was a single letter from the Cantor Fitzgerald financial management firm, which had its offices on the 101st Floor. They lost 658 employees in the terror attacks of 9/11— no survivors. I looked at the letter lying on the ground only partially covered in ash, and thought about those people, and all of those who had been killed in the attacks.

As we walked around the perimeter of the Pile, there were no landmarks. I had no bearings, no sense of direction or familiarity of a landmark. Then I finally spotted something recognizable—St. Paul's Chapel loomed unscathed, like a single tree with all of its branches and greenery following a nuclear blast. The church stood intact—all of its windows and decorations were untouched. Even the few trees on the small lot were intact, although jacketed with dust and ash. Church Street and Vessey—I now had a point of reference.

As we walked through the bombed out area I could see the damage firsthand done to the World Trade Center. Everyone had heard how the Twin Towers had been completely destroyed, but I was nearly surprised to see the vast amount of damage done to the remaining buildings in the World Trade Center complex. There would be no salvaging most of the legendary buildings.

* * *

I was different—there was no doubt about that. I sometimes felt like I was adopted—not blood related to anyone in my family. Not only did I not look like any of my siblings, but I didn't behave like anybody else. My natural desires and inclinations were different. It turned out that I was more like my father's side of the family—but I didn't discover that until later in life because my mother refused to tell us anything about my father or let us see that side of the family.

The one similarity I had to my mother is that I possessed her artistic side. I could draw, paint and act. My mother had been an aspiring actress, but never really enjoyed much success. When I came along, I seemed to have inherited some of those genes. I could draw—well; and I could paint. I had even been allowed to take advanced art classes that were reserved for the older students in high school. In college, I was asked to put on an art exhibition of my work. My mother decided I should not be so artistically inclined, and I often wondered why she felt that way.

My mother was quite bright and started college at 15, and if not for her mental challenges, I have no doubt she would have led a very successful and fulfilling life. I learned later that she left college to marry her first husband; the father of my half-sister and half-brother. After her divorce from her first husband, my mother got a job working for the New York State Department of Labor. It was there that my cousin, on my father's side, came to visit her, to inform her that my father had been killed. I later learned that he was stabbed in the chest and murdered while defending a friend.

My mother came home and told us about my father. She was very dry and matter-of-fact—"Your dad is dead." I wanted to go to his funeral, but she told me, "Absolutely not!" I was only 12. I was furious. I had never known my father, and now I never would. I did not even know what he looked like until I eventually found a photo of him, when I was 17. I was always curious about my father, and was intrigued enough to start reaching out and doing my own investigation, and learned that everything my mother had told me about my father in his family was a lie.

Our junior high and high school were combined into one big school. My mother qualified for government assistance— even though she was working, we were still hovering near poverty. I was embarrassed that I had to take a handout and came from a broken home. When you are embarrassed you tend to avoid eye contact and talk in a low voice. Looking back, I wonder if the school would have characterized me as being "on the spectrum" because of my low key avoidance of others. Because I was so different than my family, I felt like an outsider at home, and because I was on the outskirts of nice American-dream family oriented society, I felt like an outsider in public.

In high school I developed my talent, not only for drawing and painting, but for acting as well. Anything to escape. I even tried signing up for shop class and auto mechanics, but I was told shop was for boys, and I was forced to take home economics. Little tomboy denied! I was disappointed because I had been fixing up stuff around our dilapidated life since I could remember. I liked learning how things worked and putting them together the right way. I still do, and I perform some of the handyman duties around my own house.

I was in many of the plays in high school, but unfortunately for me, many were musicals, and I could not sing. I was a really bad singer; nails on the chalkboard bad. However, I would still be cast in the ensemble or small parts without a solo because I could act and move well onstage. It was a great feeling to be in front of a crowded auditorium and receive applause and kudos. That was something I never got at home—that was for damn sure.

As a result of my father's untimely death, my twin and I learned that we would be receiving Social Security benefits. My mother intercepted the early payments, and spent them on her weekends away, or other frivolous things. I felt strongly that the money should go toward my education. Her behavior was disappointing, but old news to us. In order for me to gain control of those benefits, I learned that I had to be enrolled in college by the coming January, which was six months earlier than my actual high school graduation. Luckily for us, there were a few others in the same situation, and our high school provided after school courses so we could complete our classes and finish our senior year early.

For me, not being the 'sit behind a desk' studious type, it was brutal. To cram my entire senior year into just a few short months I would arrive at school at around 8:00 a.m. and not go home until 7:00 p.m. Unlike my twin and my older siblings, who chose to go away to college, I chose to stay on Long Island and go to a Community College. I did not choose to stay local because I enjoyed living at home, but because I did not want to be in debt, and I knew if I went away to school it would cost me for many years to come. I decided I would find a way to spend more time out of the house than in it. I would eventually spend most of my time on campus or at my job flipping burgers at Burger King.

Remaining at my mother's house while attending Community College made higher education possible, financially, but it came at a price. It was an emotional nightmare dealing with all of her shit. I put myself through college flipping burgers and doing whatever job that needed to be done at the fast food joint. I worked 50 to 60 hours a week and attended college full time. I finally put enough money together to buy my mother's Buick. The Buick was not my first choice—it took me almost two years to get the stench of cigarette smoke out of the upholstery. The Buick was always on the edge of life support and I had to keep a screwdriver nearby to open the choke on the carburetor when it would refuse to start. It was a heavy load to bear, but my goal was to make enough money and get out of my mother's house.

Around the time of my high school graduation my mother suggested that I should accompany her on a vacation to Europe. A week in Greece and a week in Italy. I had to get my own passport if I wanted to go. I assumed it was my reward for graduating high school. I truly believed my mother never thought I would. I was often amazed at my mother's almost split personality between her manic and depressive phases of her bipolar illness. It was wonderful week in Greece. There was a museum near the hotel that was celebrating a "Salute to Broadway." When you walked into the museum you were greeted by our national anthem, a large American flag and a portrait of then President Ronald Reagan. It was all about the Broadway shows from New York City. In Greece, they were very serious about their beaches, with beautiful white sand and clear water. When some of the locals found out that I was from Long Island, they inquired about Jones Beach, and if I knew it, and had been there. Indeed, Jones Beach adorns the South Shore of Long Island and is one of the bigger beaches, and is really quite beautiful. Apparently, Jones Beach had worldwide notoriety.

After Greece, we spent a week in Italy. We went to many of the touristy spots like the Colosseum and Florence, among others. My mother spoke many languages and knew how to ask for out of the way places and restaurants that most tourists never see. This is where I got my first taste for travel.

I signed up for the Associate of Arts degree at the community college. I was quite content taking all of the art classes, along with acting, English and other liberal arts classes. I was a poet; a regular little bohemian, really artsy— and like most young artsy types, I had a pretty liberal view of the world and politics. As Winston Churchill declared, "'If you are not a liberal when you are young, you have no heart," and I certainly had a lot of heart. Of course, with the realities of life, like learning to balance a checkbook and seeing how the dole inculcates dependence on government handouts, I matured and transformed over the years, especially after college, interacting with people in the community and the legal system, and learning to appreciate the perfect balance between personal liberty and collective needs as outlined so wisely in the U.S. Constitution. The founders of our nation were great people, and don't let anyone tell you differently.

Speaking of my appreciation for older men . . . I found that I was attracted to mature men while I attended community college. Daddy issues? Go figure. I flirted with the idea of dating one of my college professors, and it was just a little scandalous. At least my mother thought so. She thought I should see a therapist to see if my attraction to older men might have something to do with growing up in a home . . . allow me to complete her thought, in a home where there was no stable male, and where she brought home every Tom's Harry Dick (did I get those right?) she came across. While my friends were reading Teen magazine and swooning over the latest teen heartthrob, I was watching "The Odd Couple" and "Quincy, M.E." Yep, I loved me some Jack Klugman. Okay—I admit that I may have stalked him just a little; but he enjoyed our couple of conversations, I swear. In fact, Mr. Klugman enjoyed a near photographic memory, and when he spotted me nearby at the racetrack on a few occasions, he invited me over to join him and talk about the horses. He owned a few racehorses himself. We actually met and chatted on a few occasions, always with his permission. He was always a perfect gentleman and a bright conversationalist. Yep. Jack. Actually, his TV show inspired me to want to become a medical examiner, but unfortunately, I had the brain of an artist, and couldn't get past chemistry.

In college I minored in acting as part of my liberal arts degree, and decided to audition for a play. The play was "Uncommon Women and Others," written by Wendy Wasserstein—a wonderful playwright. The play only had seven characters, so there would be a lot of competition for a part. "This is not high school!" my mother rebuffed. "You're not going to get a part. What are you—crazy?!"

Good ol' Mom. Always supportive. Always there for me when . . . oh, bullshit. When she learned I was cast to be in the play she said nothing, and I could see it didn't sit well with her. She never came to see any of my performances—not even at the college level. Wendy Wasserstein came to see the performance. She visited with us backstage afterward and told us seven performers that it was the best rendition of her play that she had ever seen. I got the distinct feeling that my mother felt that her own glory had been robbed, and she never reached her potential. As I enjoyed the successes that had eluded her, it was a biting reminder of what she had missed. That's how I read the situation.

I received a surprisingly good education during my Associate Degree program. When I eventually went to get my four-year degree, I recognized a couple of the professors who had taken classes at the Community College I had gone to. When I graduated from community college, I thought about calling it 'good enough,' but my mother told me that if I walked away from education, I'd need to find another place to live. Hmmm, I thought—"that's inconvenient." I had begun to act in regional theater, but I could tell that waiting tables was the probable outcome of that path. I didn't yet have a backup plan, so I decided to just soldier on and get my Bachelor's degree.

A local university was the natural choice, because it was close by and a great school. They were going to accept most of my credits from the Community College. However, the staff and student body were serious people, academically and socially. They were made up of people who sprang from strong, conservative families; especially on Long Island. As I said, I was a sort of hippy dippy bohemian poet, and wasn't really that university material. However, I had been an A student in my Associate's program, and they did have a great Bachelor of Arts Degree program, as long as I majored in English. So that's what I did. There was a lot of Shakespeare and literature, and so much essay writing. When I eventually went into police work, my ability to write a coherent statement really helped me.

I was young for a junior—18. It didn't affect my performance though. And, now that I was an 'adult,' I could make some of my own financial decisions and get a better job. Although credit cards had been around for a while, they were being offered to university students specifically, and it was the first time I had really given credit cards much thought. I reasoned that with better credit and a better job I would be one step closer to getting out of my mother's house.

I was 20 when I graduated with my Bachelor's Degree, and my mother said that now that I had my degree and I was an adult, I could start paying rent. Ha! Fuck that. I was the only one still living at home. My older siblings were living out of state and my twin continued on with his education and never came home. I was not willing to pay for the privilege of being psychologically tortured by my mother. No, thank you, Ma'am.

I was making decent money for that time. I was very good at my job and loved it. My art classes and my flair for color came in handy when designing floor plans for outfits and what went with them. One of the perks of working there was following and understanding the life cycle of fashions. Because I was a tomboy, I actually like sporting some of the men's extra-small, extra hip clothes. (Think colored bleached denim pants and tops). I would wait until everyone bought out the normal sizes then the company would drastically drop the price of what was left over, and I would get them at a fraction of the price. Score! I even got to cater to some Long Island local celebrities. In fact, Debbie Gibson's sister came in to purchase clothing from me for her backup band.

I was in a number of plays after I graduated from college, and worked off-off Broadway for a few years. I kept my Chess King day job during this time. Some of the acting opportunities I got were sort of substantial for a girl from the suburbs. I began going into the city to seek various acting jobs. I actually paid the bills for a while with "extra" work—you know, all of those scenes in TV shows and movies where there are people milling around in the background. If you look close enough, you'll see young Stacey Goodman walking briskly or laughing over an ice cream cone behind the stars. Oh yeah, that's me eating a sandwich on a bench as De Nero walks by. Big star!

The funny thing for me is that I started getting cast as a cop—especially in stage plays. My stature was small, but my persona was gritty. I tried out for the female version of The Odd Couple, and was cast as Murray the Cop. The actors' union gave me a certificate to go to a police supply store and purchase a police uniform. I picked up an official holster and slid my stage revolver right in. I knew I needed to get some head shots, and especially a promo shot of me in my uniform, so I put it on and stood in front of my full-length mirror and said, "Oh my god—that is me. This is what I want to be for the rest of my life." I wanted to be a cop.

After a few years of working at Chess King and being in a long term committed relationship, I became exhausted with the routine of life, and felt a deep void. I keenly felt something was missing. Chess King offered me the District Manager position, but I needed to give acting a real shot, so I decided to go in a different direction. And for reasons that still elude me, I wanted, no, *needed* to make a bigger change in my life, and I ended my romantic relationship. It was hard—for both of us. He didn't understand, and neither did I. Our friends didn't understand, and they blamed me, and I lost some of those long term friendships as well. I quit my career at Chess King and followed my heart into acting—which means I was waitressing on the side to pay the bills. I worked at TGI Friday's, and was almost surprised to find I made more money now than I was in my leadership role at Chess King.

* * *

September 11, 2001 — 06:20

Islamic extremists and members of the al-Qaida terror group Hamza al-Ghamdi and Ahmed al-Ghamdi took a taxi from their hotel to Logan International Airport, arriving at the United Airlines counter at 6:20 a.m. They both asked to purchase tickets for Flight 175 to Los Angeles, even though they already had paper tickets for the flight. They seemed preoccupied and had difficulty answering the standard security questions the counter agent asked them. They went through the questions a few times, and the agent finally gave them the go ahead. The hijacker pilot, Marwan al-Shehhi, arrived at 6:45 and checked a bag, and Islamic terrorists Fayez Banihammad and Mohand al-Shehri, checked in at 6:53.

United Flight 175 First Officer Michael Horrocks, a former marine corps pilot, called home just before he walked onto the plane, to wake his nine-year-old daughter for school. They chatted, then he looked at his watch and said, "I gotta get going now. I love you to the moon and back."

The terrorist team was led by Marwan al-Shehhi, from the United Arab Emirates. Shehhi had attended a flight training school in Florida, along with Flight 11 hijacker Mohamed Atta and Flight 93 hijacker Ziad Jarrah. Shehhi and the other four hijackers boarded United Flight 175, starting at 7:23 a.m., with Banihammad boarding first and sitting in first class seat 2A. Mohand al-Shehri sat next to him in 2B, and a couple of minutes later Shehhi and Ahmed al-Ghamdi walked onto the plane and sat in business class seats 6C and 9D, followed immediately by terrorist Hamza al-Ghamdi, who took a seat in 9C. They were in position, with their newly purchased pocketknives at the ready.

United Flight 175 was scheduled to depart for Los Angeles at 8:00 a.m. In all, 51 passengers and the five hijackers were on board, along with nine crew members. The crew included Captain Victor Saracini, First Officer Michael Horrocks, and flight attendants Robert Fangman, Amy Jarret, Amy King, Kathryn Laborie, Alfred Marchand, Michael Tarrou, and Alicia Titus.

The Captain was a former Navy Pilot, and was affectionately known as the "Forrest Gump Captain," because he would often entertain passengers with memorized movie dialogue. In addition to the terrorists on board, the other passengers included 35 men, 12 women, and three children who were under the age of five. It was a light load, at about a third of capacity.

The plane pushed away from the gate two minutes early, and was wheels up from runway 9 at 8:14 a.m. They enjoyed the summer views from the windows and reached their cruising altitude of 31,000 feet by 8:33. At 8:37 the pilots received a cryptic request from the air traffic controllers, who asked if they could see American Airlines Flight 11. They told air traffic control that they could see Flight 11, just below them, and the controllers instructed Flight 175 to turn out of the way to avoid the wayward aircraft. "Yeah, we heard a suspicious transmission from Flight 11 at takeoff. Sounds like someone keyed the mic and said 'Everyone, stay in your seats.'"

As the United Flight 175 pilots were looking back trying to see why American Airlines Flight 11 was heading in the wrong direction, terrorists Banihammad and al-Shehri forced their way into the cockpit and struggled with the pilots, killing both, while the al-Ghamdis commanded the passengers and crew to get to the back of the plane. Marwan al-Shehhi took the controls and began turning the plane around.

Chapter 3 — Headquarters

As the D.M.O.R.T. authorities walked up to us I saw some firefighters and police officers going through piles of rubble a little way off. They weren't saying much, just busily going about their task of finding the living, if there were any. The dead were just as hard to locate.

D.M.O.R.T. (Disaster Mortuary Operations Response Team), at that time, was a federal government volunteer agency comprised mostly of medical professionals who volunteered for large scale man-made and natural disasters. Most of these teams were set up around the country and could deploy quickly.

We walked around to get our bearings and in the distance saw what was left of a lifeless firehouse attached to a windowless two-story Burger King. On the side of the Burger King someone had spray painted, POLICE HEADQURTERS. I took a deep breath and let it out slowly.

Just in front of One World Financial over near the pier was the 10-story glass dome. Inside the glass was the winter garden atrium, where rows of tall palm trees invited weary winter visitors to sit among the tropical plants and dream of warmer days. It always pretended vast wealth and success of the American and global financial system. Not today. Most of the glass was blown out, leaving the skeletal metal structure.

Leading to the tall glass doors was a wide flat marble pavement.

The feds had brought in our sister disaster response organization, the Disaster Medical Assistance Teams (D.M.A.T.), to assist in the grim task of setting up our emergency morgue. The D.M.O.R.T. leader decided that the flat, fairly smooth pavement was the best place for moving around our equipment. It was a large enough space to be divided into partitioned sections—most importantly, the staging area where the remains could be kept from public view in a dignified manner until they were ready to be brought into the morgue processing area where the Medical Examiner could work on them.

Because I was a police officer and not a medical professional, my job was logistics. I was the Logistics Coordinator and my responsibilities varied, including making sure the medical staff had all the supplies they needed. I generally assisted them in whatever they needed. I also acted as liaison to other agencies. I was sworn in as a temporary federal agent, and the NYPD placed an active NYPD Lieutenant under my command.

The tents were set up and barricades maneuvered around the temporary morgue for security and privacy. Special federal I.D. badges were issued to us and had to be displayed prominently on your outer garment. This was a federal crime scene and it was imperative that the evidence be properly preserved, and the dignity of the victims be strictly observed at all times. I met with the Medical Examiner and staff that I would be working with in the temporary morgue. Some came from different D.M.O.R.T. regions, so I had never seen them before. We had a few minutes to chat and get to know each other before we went to work. The Medical Examiner was kind and, I would learn" You know," he said softly, "this is a crime scene, and you are a police officer, so when they bring in remains, you will be required to do the preliminary identification." That one sentence shook me; the weight of that responsibility was enormous, but I was up to the task.

* * *

When I was in my mid-twenties, my mother was diagnosed with severe emphysema. I thought it seemed like a good time to make peace—amends perhaps for all that had gone on in the past. She said she was going to Paris, and that a friend who was supposed to go with her cancelled at the last minute. I had no idea how bad her condition was or if this would be the last time we could travel together, so I said I would go. I thought it would be a good opportunity for us to finally get to know one another at a mother-daughter level; something we'd never really had.

The guy I was with at that time took my going to Paris with my ailing mother as a personal affront to his needs and wants, and that relationship spiraled downward after that. My mother had been to Paris before and knew many out of the way spots that tourists seldom go. We enjoyed good local cuisine and had a couple of heart to heart conversations, including the one about her old friend Jack.

One night, I decided to try the nightlife at the suggestion of the hotel concierge. I was directed to a club on the other side of the city. I got on the train across the street from the hotel, which lets you off down the block from the club. I had a great time and met a wonderful Spanish family. Entire families would often go to the clubs in Europe as one big group. Before I knew it, it was 2:00 a.m. and I thought I should get back to the hotel. I stepped outside and the streets were empty. There were no cabs, no buses, no cars—no one. I asked someone about it, who told me that all transportation had stopped running at midnight. Good to know.

Unlike today, there were no cellphones or driving services. I decided to walk back to the hotel. What could possibly go wrong with that decision? I set out following the train track back in the direction of my hotel. As I walked along in the dark the thought occurred to me that the hotel might have a shuttle or hotel guests car service for just such an occasion. I wish I'd thought of that earlier.

I heard footsteps behind me and I took a quick glance back and saw two young men. "Oh shit," I whispered, thinking that I might end up a dead American in Paris. I walked faster, and the footsteps got closer, and then the men finally caught up to me.

I braced myself for whatever might come next, and heard one of them say in excellent English, "Are you American?"

I stopped and turned around, getting ready to rumble. "Yeah," I replied.

"What are you doing out here in the middle of the night alone?" he asked.

It was a great question. "I didn't know the cabs, buses and trains all stopped running at midnight," I replied. "I thought it was like New York City."

The men glanced at each other. "Which hotel are you staying at?" one asked. I told them. "Do you mind if we walk with you? It can be dangerous for a woman to be alone out here in the middle of the night."

That much I'd figured out. "Thank you," I said, and they walked me all the way back to the hotel. I was lucky. I turned out to be a little less street savvy than I thought. That was true, at least, when I got a little out of my native element. Another life lesson learned.

* * *

September 11, 2001 — 07:15

At 7:15 a.m., al-Qaida Islamic terrorists Khalid al-Mihdhar and Majed Moqed checked in at the American Airlines ticket counter at Dulles International Airport for Flight 77 to Los Angeles. When they arrived at the passenger security checkpoint a few minutes later, they both set off the metal detector, and were escorted through secondary screening. Moqed set off the second alarm, and was additionally searched with a hand wand.

Brothers, Nawaf and Salem al-Hazmi checked in together at 7:29. Trained and certified pilot Hani Hanjour checked in by himself, and arrived at the security checkpoint at 7:35. As the al-Hazmi brothers attempted to get through the security checkpoint, they also set off the alarm on the metal detector. The screener at the checkpoint searched them, but never figured out what was triggering the alarm.

The hijackers were all selected for extra security screening of their checked bags as well, because they were deemed suspicious by the check-in agent. They made it through security however, and walked to Gate D26 to await boarding.

The five terrorist hijackers boarded the aircraft with the other 53 passengers, consisting of 26 men, 22 women, and five children ranging in age from three to eleven. Among the passengers was Barbara Olson, the wife of the United States Solicitor General Theodore "Ted" Olson, who was traveling to appear on the TV show "Politically Incorrect." A group of three

11-year-old children, along with their chaperones, plus two National Geographic Society staff members were also on board.

Hani Hanjour took his seat in first class, 1B, and the al-Hazmi brothers sat close behind him in seats 5E and 5F. Majed Moqed and Khalid al-Mihdhar sat together farther back, in economy class, in seats 12A and 12B.

American Airlines Flight 77 was scheduled to depart at 8:10, and the plane pushed back from the gate on time and headed for runway 30, and lifted off the runway at 8:20.

Less than 35 minutes after leaving Dulles the terrorists stormed the cockpit. They forced the pilots out, and moved them to the back of the plane with the crew and passengers. Hani Hanjour, took control of the aircraft and the other four hijackers guarded the passengers and crew.

Chapter 4 — Take My Breath Away

It was decided by those in charge that the temporary morgue would be set up on the street side of One World Financial Center. It made the most sense because it was in close proximity to the main dig Pile. The area just outside the main doorway was made up of a mostly smooth pavement which would make it easy to move around. A statue that stood in front of the large glass doorway had to be removed. The tents were set up and barricades put in place. During my first work shift, and every one after that, I made it my business to be sure that the medical staff had all the supplies set up and ready for when they needed them. I have always been a big proponent of organization. I kept a tidy and organized home and was often playfully teased by friends and other cops that I was the O.C.D. Queen, because I was super organized. Here, I could put my skills to good use. I made sure all the gloves were available and placed in size order. No job was too big or too small. I procured a mop and bucket to clean whatever dust had been tracked in during the day, in the hope of preserving a respectful atmosphere and maintaining a safe work environment.

The feds delivered a number of large, heavy duty polyethylene storage containers, and we opened them and found hundreds of 3M multipurpose respirators that were huge, bulky masks with separate filters that attached on either side of the rubber nose and mouthpiece. I looked at them, and thought of movies were the heroes wore them to avoid biohazards. Let me say, they looked hideous, and ominous, but I had to smile at the bright pink filter casing.

We were told to wear the masks and keep them on, and to change the filters daily. I grabbed a mask and a pair of filters, and they were huge, awkward, heavy masks. I was small and the mass seemed too big for my little face. I had to have one of the doctors show me how to properly wear the mask by adjusting the straps and creating a tight seal. I got the mask to fit but now the rubber straps were longer and flopping around. I did not like that. Not at all. It looked horrible. It felt horrible. I looked like in the evil chainsaw-wielding character from a horror movie. However, I understood that we were in the middle of a toxic Pile full of asbestos in all kinds of lowest bidder shit, and it was swirling up into our lungs with each breath. I wore the mask. It was bulky and uncomfortable. It was ugly. Many of the others in my area didn't wear them. Most of the firefighters didn't wear them; they said they took their breath away. Even some of the doctors and other medical staff laughed at how ridiculous I looked in my giant mask. They didn't mock me for wearing it, but only laughed at how silly I looked. One of the doctors candidly told me, "You'll be the only one of us alive in 20 years." The other doctors said the same thing to me. I laughed at their jokes, but twenty years have gone by fast, and indeed, the irony is that they were right. Despite my difficulties, I've outlived many of them, and only time will tell who will be the last man standing.

The first couple of days there was no running water, so porta potties were brought in and bottled drinking water was delivered. Private people and large companies were donating necessary supplies like water, hard hats, goggles and even boots. Everyone was an American in the days following 9/11 2001, and even the media pitched in by getting the word out on supplies that were needed at Ground Zero. Bottled water, plus specialized items like protective clothing and leather gloves were in high demand, because shards of glass, cement and steel poked through the debris.

The entire area around the Pile was deemed unstable until investigators and building inspectors could gain access to the structures to determine if any would be salvageable. We were told motion sensors were put on many of the buildings around the Pile that were accessible. They were unstable, and they told us that if the alarms went off, *run!*

After a few days running water was restored to the atrium building behind the temporary morgue, and the restroom inside became available once the building inspectors said that section of One World Financial was stable enough to enter. A Red Cross volunteer was assigned to the area and he set up a cot between the men's room and the women's room. He was there every night, sleeping in his cot. If one of us walked back to use the restrooms, he was up and ready to get us anything we needed. I would try to tiptoe around to avoid disturbing him, but there was no sneaking by him. He would happily jump up and ask if there was anything we needed, or anything he could do for us. He swept and mopped, and kept the soap and paper supplies topped off at all times. He was a delightful man, and did everything he could to make our service easier. I have always said of that man, and every other volunteer and worker on the Pile no matter what service was rendered, "He's as much a hero as anyone out there."

※ ※ ※

After my 'revelation' of sorts, that my destiny was to serve and protect, my first step was to join the Nassau County Auxiliary Police. It was a volunteer service and I thought it would be a great way to see if law enforcement would be a good fit for me. The auxiliary police fell under the Emergency Management of Nassau County, which was run by both civilians and sworn police officers. The main responsibilities were to do routine patrols in marked vehicles and report anything that was worth reporting to the Nassau County police via a police radio. The auxiliary police was responsible for assisting with street fairs, parades, traffic control, and basically whatever the real police needed assistance with.

My first step was to be interviewed by the police officer in charge of the Auxiliary Police. Ray was a Nassau County police officer who handled all the day-to-day operations of the auxiliary police, and as I would later find out, was going through a divorce. Of course, he met all of my criteria for a desirable man—he was mature and had some authority. Don't get me wrong, I do not mean to say I was looking for power or to sleep my way to the top. I mean my visceral response to a man like him was to be attracted. However, maturity and power aren't all they are cracked up to be, so let me be clear that my roster of boyfriends from that time forward was fairly lackluster.

I passed my background check, made it through the civilian Police Academy and graduated top of my class. I was assigned to a unit close to my home and felt I was ready to take the flurry of exams necessary to become a real police officer.

I decided I should get all the law-enforcement wannabe jobs. I phased out of my TGI Friday's gig and became the female version of Paul Blart, mall cop—well, more like mall security guard. I worked in the Roosevelt Field Mall, a mix of the very wealthy and very poor; quite the combustible combination. Nassau County had set up in a mini detection area for shoplifters when the mall was remodeled. The Nassau officers knew that I was an Auxiliary Officer and they were always looking out for me. The guys knew I was taking tests to get on the job, and when they needed someone to help them with something they would ask me, due to my pre-Academy training. The two men who ran the security company were retired NYPD detectives. They liked me because I was a hard worker and took instruction well. The job was only part-time, however, and I knew I needed to get a full-time gig to bring in some more money.

My mother worked for the New York State Department of Labor for over 30 years and had just retired. She actually suggested on numerous occasions that I take a civil service job like she had, so when big companies like Pan Am airlines went out of business in December of 1991, the Department of Labor needed to hire quickly for labor service reps to find replacements for all those people. Unlike today, back then not everything was done via computer. I was able to get into professional placement, which was where I met my friend Gina. We did not mix well at first, but then became inseparable. Gina and I helped each other get better at our jobs and before we knew it, some of the older employees were pissed at us for overperforming and making them look like the underachievers they were. That was not our intention—but excellence necessarily stirs the ire of the indolent. It got to the point that more experienced visitors would ask for one of us to assist them.

The other employees liked it when we would be sent to on-site work fairs. No one else wanted the assignment, and we gladly took it. Internet jobsites had not taken off back then, so we would sit at our booth at new business openings and help people apply for jobs at that business. Big retailers, for instance, would need dozens of new employees, and would have trouble getting the target prospects in for an interview. That's where we came in. We prescreened potential matches for interviews with the managers, and filled their schedules with quality candidates. It was a win-win.

The Department of Labor office was located in a very rough part of Freeport. Violent crimes were committed there daily. There were shootings and every crime imaginable so we had to have a security guard at the door. He was a marine, so I felt safe. Freeport had its own Police Department and they often worked with the Nassau County Police, so the guys would come in to check on me from time to time. It made some of the other employees wonder about me, and they wanted to know why the police were stopping by to talk with me. Nothing like making friends at work.

I became a trusted member of the Auxiliary Police and devoted a lot of time to it. I rose to the rank of Lieutenant, and was transferred to the Headquarters unit. I became so good at traffic control, some of the Police Academy staff thought it would be a great idea for me to teach real police recruits how it was done.

Being a member of the Auxiliary Police opened a few doors for me, so when the recession hit and all the provisional employees were laid off from the Department of Labor, Ray suggested that I interview for the Red Cross position that had just become available. It did not pay well, but with a job title like Disaster Specialist, it was right up my alley! The Nassau County police gave me a glowing recommendation and I was hired. I was trained to handle plane crashes and other disasters, like floods, fires, earthquakes, hurricanes, and anything else that could bring devastation to the people of the region.

I met an older woman who was an accountant at the Red Cross, who was looking for a tenant for the second floor of her two story home in Williston park. I happened to be looking for an apartment at the time so I took a look at her place. It was a small one bedroom one bath with a small living room and she was not asking very much. There was no kitchen. Good; I did not like to cook much anyway.

I was working for the Red Cross for only a few months when my landlady came to me—visibly upset and shaken. She said, "I think there's a problem."

"What kind of problem?" I asked.

"I'm really afraid."

"Tell me," I said, "because I'm not afraid. What's going on?"

"Money is missing," she said. "Lots of money is missing." I knew she worked in the accounting department, and I knew she was very good at her job, and meticulously honest.

To me, it was evident that money was being misappropriated. "Okay, then. Let's blow the whistle and bring down the thieves who're stealing from the Red Cross."

"But I'm pretty sure it's our boss, Dee," she said.

I looked at her evidence, and it was clear that the boss was embezzling funds from the organization. Tens of thousands of dollars were clearly misappropriated. "Okay," I said. "Your evidence is solid. Let's roll with it."

Despite her trepidation, I marshalled all of the evidence and put together a letter explaining what she had discovered as an accounting department employee, and sent it to the National Red Cross Chapter that overlooks all the local chapters, and requested an audit to be performed. Shortly thereafter, I was suddenly relieved of my duties—fired—my 'thanks' for being a whistleblower. It was a retaliatory strike from Dee, my direct boss. My whistleblower landlady got a pink slip as well. That was it. Another retaliatory strike.

The National Chapter came in, did the audit and found discrepancies, and the culprits were fired, including my direct boss. I walked away and didn't look back, and picked up as many hours as I could from my side gigs. Within a couple of months I got word that Dee had been fired from the Red Cross, and that my landlady had gotten her job back. Shortly thereafter I received a call thanking me for my courage, and offering me my position back as well. I thanked them, but said I had moved on.

I continued to live in that same apartment for a few more years.

* * *

On December 7th, 1993, Colin Ferguson boarded the Long Island Railroad commuter train that left Penn Station and headed east, bringing city workers back to their homes on Long Island. When the train eased into the Merillon Avenue stop in Garden City, Ferguson used a Ruger P89 9mm semi-automatic handgun to shoot and kill six people and seriously wound 19 others.

I was one of a few Nassau County Auxiliary Police officers to be asked to assist with the traffic control. Garden City had their own small Police Department and relied heavily on the Nassau County Police to handle large crime scenes. I was given a traffic post a few blocks from the incident to divert traffic away from the scene. While at my post, I noticed a middle aged man walking in the street, and he appeared confused to me. I watched him a moment, and could see he was in shock. I guided him out of the middle of the roadway and asked some basic questions, which he could not readily answer. I had him sit in my vehicle as I radioed the Nassau County Police to respond.

Police detectives were sent to my car, and they interviewed the man, and determined that he had witnessed the shootings on the train. A nearby Garden City police officer saw that I had brought in Nassau County detectives to interview the dazed man, and got in my face for not notifying him first. He brutalized me, and went up one side of me and down the other. A Nassau County police officer saw what he was doing, and dressed him down—in front of me. He then told the cop to take over my traffic control post, and I was personally escorted back to the crime scene by one of the detectives that knew I was on the Suffolk County list to be hired.

He took me to the inner perimeter of the crime scene. I could see the train from where I was, and I could see the blood on the windows and floor of the train car. It surprised me to see that the blood was so thick that it looked like red curtains on the windows.

Chapter 5 — First Hero

We were still setting up when I heard a sound behind me from the entry into the temporary morgue. I turned to see who was coming in and I was a little surprised to find a small group of firefighters. They were covered in ash and dust and looked very tired—exhausted. They each looked at me and I wondered what they were doing inside the morgue, seeing it was such a high security area. I had seen many firefighters working on the Pile, but somehow never expected to encounter them inside the morgue. Then I realized they were carrying a rescue basket. No one said a word as I watched them place their brother firefighter onto the steel examination table. They stood, helmets removed in respect, next to their fallen brother. This was our first victim.

All of the setting up, organizing, prepping; and now it was beginning. I glanced back up at the firefighters, their somber looks made all the sense in the world to me now. I pursed my lips, and glanced over as I saw the Medical Examiner slowly donning a pair of latex gloves. The M.E. walked over to the examination table. The firefighters stepped out of the examination tent, except for one, who had gone over to the police officer sitting on a stool in the corner to record all that transpired, giving him information about the deceased. Then he followed the other firefighters out of the examination tent. I stood across from the M.E. and looked down at the lifeless body that was on the steel table. He was in full turn out gear, and still had his dual tank Scott Air Pak beneath him. Most likely he had run into one of the burning towers while people were running out. He climbed the stairs with over 75 pounds of gear on his back. His Scott Air Pak had been crushed flat. I shudder to think of the crushing impact that had killed him and was relieved that his body did not reflect that degree of violence. I could see the heavy coat of gray ash everywhere on his lifeless body. He had a handsome young face and his dust covered eyelids were closed.

I looked up at the others. *Are they waiting for me?* I thought to myself. The M.E. and the police officer in the corner taking meticulous notes just looked at the table. I was uncomfortable— *Are they waiting for me?* I repeated. My lips were dry; my nose and eyes were burning. I thought for a moment. The M.E. had told me that my main job was to perform preliminary I.D. on the deceased as they came in. The firefighter had given the recorder the deceased man's name and battalion number. There wasn't much left for me to do. It was then that I realized they were taking a moment out of respect for the fallen hero.

I stood silently waiting for instruction as the M.E. completed his preliminary exam. He stepped away from the table and removed his gloves. The recorder followed the M.E. as he stepped out of the examination tent to the hand washing station in the adjacent tent. I was alone in the examination tent with the fallen hero. As I surveyed him from head to toe, my mind filled with thoughts of all the police officers and firefighters who ran up those staircases into the face of danger in an effort to save hundreds, if not thousands of lives—many of whom were trapped by fire, and without help would never live to see loved ones again. These brave men and women made the ultimate sacrifice, and now I would begin to meet them in this most solemn of duties.

I looked down at him one more time and noticed his bulky uniform was twisted and his arm was hanging off the table—he seemed undignified that way. I stepped forward and gently lifted his arm back onto the table and laid it by his side. I straightened his uniform. It was then that I noticed the firefighters had returned to the examination tent. They stood like silent sentinels watching as I paid my respects to their fallen brother.

I stepped back sheepishly. They had been watching me and I was not sure for how long. One of the firefighters was clutching an American flag as they stepped forward. He looked at me. "Would you like to help us?" he gestured while unfurling the flag.

"I would be honored," I replied and took a step forward beside the firefighters as they placed the lifeless body back into the rescue basket. They handed me the edge of the flag and I reached over and took it. Together we lowered the flag over the body and tucked it in gently around him. We all stood in silence for a moment, then the firefighters lifted the basket one last time and carried their fallen brother to the waiting ambulance. They slid the basket into the back of the ambulance and I watched as they swung the doors closed. I didn't move as the ambulance pulled away and ambled through the cleared pavement leaving swirls of dust in its wake.

I walked back into the morgue and found the M.E. standing inside, and I asked where the bodies were being taken. He said all remains would go to the New York City Medical Examiner's Office, up on 26th Street. Families would be informed, arrangements would be made. It was far from routine, but it would be repeated hundreds of times in the coming weeks. I took a deep breath through my bulky mask, and fought back tears at the realization of such tremendous loss, then turned and walked back, getting everything ready for the next victim.

███

I finally received a letter from the Suffolk County Police Department advising me that the vetting process to become a police officer would begin. I was very excited. I had taken a few entrance level exams to become a police officer for various jurisdictions, and at the ripe old age of 29, had 'aged out' of the New York State Troopers. Now, this was my shot. I had focused on this opportunity and invested heavily in it for years, and now it was actually within my grasp.

I was assigned a series of tasks to complete, all while an extensive and thorough background check would be conducted. The first test I was assigned was to draw, freehand, three maps to my previous employers. I assumed this test was to determine if I could use and understand maps—no easy access to GPS back then. I was Little Miss Artist and I had an excellent sense of where things were in relation to other places. So I created beautiful 3D maps filled with detail and all of the requested and required information. There were other monotonous and uninteresting tasks that were required, and I got a quick sense that this was more of an elimination process than an actual test of skills and abilities, to weed out the lazy. That's what they were looking for—getting rid of the quitters early. I'm sure there were some candidates that said, "Fuck it. I'm not doing this," and walked away.

My police investigator was Darlene M. She was a tough cookie, and a very thorough investigator. Darlene had knocked on all my neighbors' doors and visited all the places I had worked. I was approached by one neighbor who thought I was in some kind of trouble. "The police were asking questions about you." Another neighbor asked, "Are you in trouble?" I just smiled and told them that it was part of my background check to become a police officer. I showed up at the mall for my Paul Blart duties while Darlene was there interviewing the two retired NYPD detectives who were my bosses. They loudly replied to Darlene's question, "We only have bad shit to say about Stacey, because we need her working here!" Darlene laughed, and they gave me the thumbs up. They even told her about the time or two I had assisted the Nassau County Police with their cases at the mall.

Next came the letter in the mail from the Suffolk County Police Department telling me to report at a scheduled date and time at police headquarters to take a polygraph test. Each step of the process to become a police officer was initiated by an official looking letter that would arrive at my mailbox at my apartment, telling me to report for something, or give me instructions.

I showed up at police headquarters early, dressed in business attire. They sat me down in a small, sparse room meant to intimidate me. They strapped me in, and promptly left the room. I observed a camera up in the corner and assumed they were watching me from another location. I sat still but I could feel my heart racing. I was definitely uncomfortable. The two examiners came in the room again, with one sitting in a chair that he pulled awfully close to me. "Just tell the truth," he advised. At first he asked simple questions. Just yes or no, easy ones to start. Then one of the examiners left the room again. I knew some of my answers would need some explanations other than just yes or no.

They asked about my alcohol consumption and I think they were amused by my answer. "Well, I only had one drink. It was a vodka and cranberry. I was with a friend at a bar in New York. I only drank half, because it tasted awful and it burned my throat." The examiner looked at me incredulously, then asked about drugs—if I had ever taken them or ever been around them. I'd never taken recreational drugs so that was an easy no, but the second part required a little explanation.

"Well, I was at a party with a friend and some dumb fuck took some coke out of his pocket." I said that I was out of there immediately and left the party. "The fucker was still wearing his American Airlines mechanic's overalls," I told them. I said I'd made a mental note to avoid that airline. When they were done with the questioning, they left the room again, then came back and thanked me, and said someone would be in touch. Overall, they seemed relaxed at the end and I left feeling that I had passed. A few days later I received a letter confirming that.

Next was the psych exam. This was both a written and interview exam. After taking the written portion I sat down with a woman who claimed to be best friends with—my old boss from the Red Cross. The same one who was responsible for firing me for being a whistleblower. I said nothing to this woman. I just looked at her. Was I expected to blow my top and say something stupid at this point? Bullshit. I just looked at her. I didn't flinch. Nothing. It was just bullshit and I knew it. She watched me for a minute, then moved on to something else. The various psych evaluations were grueling and lasted almost five hours. I assumed that some failed at this point, maybe told them to go fuck themselves and stormed out. Not me. I understood what they were doing, and more importantly, why they were doing it. I stayed cool the entire time. I assumed that's the characteristic they were looking for; to cull the hotheads and egomaniacs from the herd.

One day another letter showed up from the Suffolk County Police Department. "Is this it?" I said as I opened it. I hurried and took the letter out of the envelope and unfolded it with anxious hands. "Congratulations," it began.

"Holy shit!" I said loudly.

"The police Academy starts October 30, 1995." I was in seventh heaven. This was it! It said the Police Academy was six months long, every Monday through Friday. We received a small salary while we attended, and it was just enough to pay for my rent and to cover my few bills.

I immediately gave my buddies at the mall notice that I could not come in any longer—they were on their own now.

I lived in Mineola and the Police Academy was at that time in Babylon. It was in an unused elementary school. As I pulled in for my first day, I was dressed in my business best and had a big smile on my face with my music going and the window down. Big mistake. A Suffolk County police officer who was in tip-top shape in his sparkling uniform started jogging next to my car, yelling at me to turn off the music and wipe that smile off my face. Awesome. It was going to be a long six months.

The Suffolk County Police Department is comprised of about 2,400 sworn police officers and covers the five western towns in Suffolk County on Long Island, New York, and serves around 1.4 million residents. There were 56 of us reporting to the Police Academy, only six of whom were women. We were all dressed like business professionals. I wore a pantsuit, and the other women wore skirts. Hell, I was not doing that. They sat us all in the tiny grade school desks. We listened intently as one of the instructors was speaking, but I must have missed something—someone sneezed or farted, and that got the instructors mad. We had to get on the floor and 'give them 20 pushups,' then stay in plank position while they yelled at us. Good times.

We were all fitted for gray uniforms. We were pond scum, and told we were not worthy of wearing the traditional police blue uniform yet. No badge, no gun, just a simple gray uniform with a plain black belt, black socks, and black shoes that we had to constantly shine. The patch worn on either side of the uniform was affectionately nicknamed "the pizza patch," because of its large size, color and . . . because it looked like a slice of pizza. We had department-issued sweats that were required for physical training. Extra-small for me, please.

I learned right away that there was no special treatment for the females. In fact, it was quite the opposite. While the men got to enjoy a break, they would take us out back and onto the field to do pushups in bird shit. We were told we were not wanted and should just quit, and leave. I was not impressed with the games and their psychological bullshit, but I played along. *I don't give a fuck. I am not quitting—you just tell me what you want me to do and I will do it*, I would say to myself, because I did not dare say it out loud. I had prepared for the intense physical training even before entering the Police Academy. Running, building upper body strength and core exercises. I enjoyed running and had been running and jogging since I was a teenager. The instructors felt I was enjoying the running too much, and pushed us. They pushed me to the point where I would run so hard I would puke. Then I'd run some more. Fuck 'em. I was being paid to run, that made me a professional athlete. Nothing could stop me from doing my job—and that was running.

They ran me so hard that I injured my foot. I said nothing to them because I didn't want to give them any ammo to shoot at me. Then one of the instructors caught me limping in the hallway. I got yelled at. "Do you think you're special? Do you require special treatment?!"

"Sir! No, Sir."

Aside from the daily grueling physical requirements, there were the mental and educational requirements. We had to earn a B average to survive. I studied a lot. All the studying, physical training and having to iron my uniform to keep the perfect crease—I would get home each night and prepare for the day, then do it all over again. I would be so tired at night I was usually in bed by 8:00 o'clock each evening.

I was small, and they complained about my weight, so I needed to eat more—bulk up. I went into the academy at 109 pounds, and I finished at 109. We only had 10 minutes for lunch each day, so I made what I could eat easy and fast—so peanut butter and jelly on whole wheat bread were on the menu every day. Some days I had two sandwiches—to try to bulk it up. After P.T. each day, we had just 10 minutes to shower and be in class, in uniform, perfectly dressed. My actress mane was slowing me down, so I cut my hair nice and short, so I wouldn't have to listen to some dumbass yelling at me that a wisp of hair was out of place. Nope—Ray was not happy when I cut my hair. Ray was less happy with each passing day.

The six months of the police academy went through an unusually bitter winter, and on the morning of a severe blizzard I looked outside and said, "No fucking way."

We had a big test scheduled that day, but I assumed it was all canceled. I called the academy just to confirm that no one was going in that day and they told me, "Police don't take snow days—because criminals don't take snow days." I was surprised that they were so gung-ho, and got bundled up and left early. I crept along in my car, trying to stay in the middle of the road, praying I wouldn't get stuck or slide off into a ditch, or worse. It was treacherous. About an hour into the drive I was almost surprised to see flashing lights in my rear view mirror, and I pulled over a little, hoping he'd go around me. Nope. He pulled up behind me and got out of his car and walked up as I rolled down my window, letting in the freezing wind.

"You know the roads are all closed today, Ma'am," he started.

"Uh, yeah, I do, Officer. But I'm in the Suffolk County Police Academy, and I called in and they told me criminals don't take snow days, so to get my ass in today."

He looked at my grays under my jacket and chuckled a little and nodded knowingly. "I see. Okay then. Just be extra careful." He let me continue my winter trek.

I made my way to the academy, and found that only about five of us had come in. They smiled at me and wrote my name down. "Okay, you can go home now. Test is tomorrow."

I got in my car and started the long drive back home. I got paid for that day, and never heard if those who didn't come in got in any sort of trouble. As far as I was concerned, only 10 percent had come in, and that put me automatically in the top 10 percent. I got home and decided I'd better read everything again for the postponed test. I slept and read, all day.

When the weather warmed up, so did the instructors. The Academy was still grueling, but at least we were not being yelled at so much. And I know, that was also part of the training. It was exciting when we finally got to go to the practice range. We had to shoot at cardboard targets that looked like milk bottles—yeah, that's realistic. At first it took me a bit to get the hang of it, but then I was shooting center mass about 80 percent of the time. When we trained on metal targets I did even better. The instructors would get on my case and want to know why. I told them it must be the instant gratification; hearing the noise it made when I hit the target.

One day while shooting at the cardboard targets, I got a weird feeling something was not right. I heard the instructors yelling for everyone to stop shooting and holster our weapons. One instructor approached me and asked me if I was okay, and told me not to move. I had no intention of moving, and was wondering what the hell was going on. Apparently, the recruit next to me hit a piece of the metal part of the stand that held his target, and a piece of shrapnel came back at me and hit my cheek. I had two instructors hovering over me. They pulled the metal from my cheek and asked if I was okay. I said yes, mainly because I was not enjoying all of the attention. I heard one of the instructors jokingly say, "I'm putting you in for a Purple Heart."

Despite all of the yelling and bullshit tactics, only a few of our number washed out. A couple did not like getting yelled at. Go figure. Another shot himself accidentally. I guess they felt he wasn't cop material. When it became apparent that I was going to graduate, Ray started acting differently. He became more distant. One day he just came out and said, "I don't like female cops."

"Well," I said, "your girlfriend is going to be one." We stayed together for a few more years, but the relationship fizzled, then faded, then went on life support. It died.

At the end of six months I was informed that I had successfully completed the Academy. The date of our graduation was set. We were allowed to invite family and friends. My brother Danny and some of my friends came. The Suffolk County Police Department welcomed the new recruits. I was assigned to the 4th precinct in Smithtown. It was where all the female prisoners from around the county were warehoused until they could be transported to the courts, so they needed female cops there.

♦ ♦ ♦

September 11, 2001 — 08:24:38

On American Airlines Flight 11, Mohamed Atta hit the microphone button to speak with the passengers on the plane, but mistakenly broadcast a message to the Boston air traffic controllers. "We have some planes. Just stay quiet and you'll be oaky. We are returning to the airport." At 08:24:56 he announced, "Nobody move. Everything will be okay. If you try to make any moves, you'll endanger yourself and the airplane. Just stay quiet."

At 8:26 a.m. Mohamed Atta turned the plane south, and a few minutes later he broadcast, "Nobody move, please. We are going back to the airport. Don't try to make any stupid moves."

At that point the pilots of United Airlines Flight 175 confirmed to air traffic control Flight 11's location and heading, who informed NORAD (North American Aerospace Defense Command) Northeast Air Defense Sector (NEADS), who called on two F-15 fighter jets at Otis Air National Guard Base in Mashpee, Massachusetts, to intercept Flight 11.

"We are in rapid descent—we are all over the place. Oh, my God, we are too low!" flight attendant Amy Sweeney exclaimed over the American Airlines emergency line.

At 8:46:30 the five Islamic terrorists intentionally slammed American Airlines Flight 11 into the northern façade of the North Tower of the World Trade Center at 465 m.p.h., hitting between floors 93 and 99, carrying 10,000 gallons of jet fuel.

The F-15s took off at 8:53 a.m., speeding to intercept the hijacked commercial jet.

Hundreds of North Tower occupants and all of those aboard Flight 11 were killed instantly at the time of initial impact. The elevator shafts channeled the burning jet fuel through the blazing Tower, exploding in the Skylobbies on floors 78 and 22, and in the main lobby at the base. The stairwells and elevators from floor 92 and up were impassable, and many hundreds of victims were unable to escape, many of them dying from smoke inhalation or flames, with several being forced by the searing heat to jump out of the windows to their death far below.

Within 102 minutes of impact, Tower One collapsed, killing occupants and many heroic first responders who were rushing upward to rescue the injured and trapped. In all, over 1,300 died in Tower One.

Chapter 6 — Bone of My Bones

I had been busy cleaning and organizing in the makeshift morgue, trying to keep busy and not think about what was happening on the outside of the tents. I turned to see an older looking man in the doorway of the examination tent and saw that he was carefully cradling something in his cupped hands. The defeated but focused look on his tired face told us that what he held was precious to him. I looked over at the door wondering how this man made his way in here. He wore no uniform or special badge, but no one had followed him in. The Medical Examiner looked over at him and I could see he was waiting for an explanation. The man was clean shaven and had a full head of white hair, and was thin and fairly tall. I estimated his age at around 65 to 70 years old. The M.E. leaned over to look in the man's cupped hands then he beckoned me over with a quick gesture. I quickly grabbed a clean pair of gloves and put them on. The M.E. had the man place what was in his hands onto the clean steel table. I could see they were bones.

"This is my son," the man said.

The M.E. looked at him a moment, then down at the handful of bones lying on the table before him. I could see portions of a tibia and what appeared to be a knee bone lying loosely on the table. The M.E. questioned, "Your son? How can you be sure?"

The man explained that he was retired FDNY and that he had volunteered to join the search and rescue teams on the Pile. "My son went missing in the South Tower," he explained, "and I thought that if there was any way to find him, I'd rather it was me."

The M.E. glanced sideways at me, then back at the suffering father. "But what makes you think these bones belong to your son?"

"You can see it in this knee. It's my son." He pointed to the knee bone and the M.E. took a closer look as the man continued to explain. "My son had this surgery on his knee. It's not very common—this metal piece here," he pointed. "This is my son."

It was somewhere around this point that my convictions told me I should say something; the compulsory, *I'm sorry for your loss.* But watching this shaken father, the veteran of a thousand tragedies in this city, stare at those stripped bones and tell us that he knew it was his son left me speechless— something that seemed nearly impossible at most points in my career as a cop. I fought back the tears that I was meticulous to hide from everyone. It was a losing battle this time. I choked to keep my emotions buried, to keep from heaping distress on the tired firefighter, or the M.E. It took all of my strength to maintain my dignified, respectful vigil.

The M.E. thanked the man, and the NYPD officer sitting in the corner took copious notes as the man relayed his son's vital information. Name, date of birth, height, hair color—not that most of that would help much at this point. When he had shared all of the pertinent information about his fallen son, the M.E. instructed him how to contact the city's Medical Examiner's office as he escorted the man out of the examination tent.

＊ ＊ ＊

I was out of the Academy setting and began my field training. Field training consisted of 10 to 12 weeks, and the first couple of those weeks you spent at an adjacent precinct. Because I was going to the 4th precinct, I spent my first couple of weeks at the third precinct. My 3rd Precinct trainer was a guy whose attitude was, *sit in the car and shut up*. Not very inspiring—and not a valuable training experience. The practice of having recruits train in a different precinct was determined to be faulty, because training officers knew that the recruit would be going to another precinct, so why put any real effort into it? The practice has since been changed. It was such a negative experience for me, it was the closest I ever came to quitting. I felt my trainer was rude and inconsiderate, and he ate every meal of his life from a fast food drive up window.

One thing that I discovered while in the Academy was that mace did not affect me as much as it did others. Sure, it wasn't pleasant, but I could blow my nose and get back into standard functioning levels without too much trouble. Others could be disabled for several minutes. It may have been related to my high pain threshold. I seemed to withstand pain better than most. I don't use pain relievers, even after major surgeries I've had. Every time a doctor would suggest I used opioids for pain, I suggested a different use for the whole bottle. On one occasion I got into a fight with a scumbag—technical legal jargon for 'criminal who resists arrest'—and it took a word from my boss for me to notice my two broken fingers.

My trainer took a call to a situation where a cop had felt threatened and loaded the house up with mace. There was a woman inside who had a warrant for her arrest, and they thought she had access to a gun, so it was better to go in right away and get her. We were standing outside the house, and the cops suddenly looked at me and one said, "Hey, you're the one who can handle mace. You're the rookie. You go in and get her out." The object of the police department was to protect the rookie—but as I mentioned, because training was conducted in different precincts than the one assigned, that didn't always take a high priority. I was sent in.

I got through the door and there were people lying on the ground inside breathing into towels, and I said, "Where's the woman?"

"The back room," they pointed without looking up.

The house was flooded with mace, and even though it didn't cripple me like it did others, it was no stroll in the park. My eyes were in searing pain. My nose and throat felt like they were on fire. I wasn't worried about the people I was passing because they were incapacitated. When they said she was in the back room, my thought was that she was probably trying to get to her gun, so I rushed to the back and broke through the door. I saw her on the far side of the bed looking around a cabinet the best she could with her arm over her eyes. I ran and took a leap and bounced off the bed and hit her hard in flight, taking her straight to the ground. When I had her under control the others came to the door and took her away, and I got some water for my eyes and blew my nose. Not a 'thank you.' Not a 'good job.' Not a word. They just took the woman into custody and drove away, like I wasn't even standing there.

I was happy when my training at the 3rd precinct was over and I could finally go to the 4th Precinct. I learned my field training officer was going to be a female and I was looking forward to training with her. However, she had just finished field training one of the guys from my class, and it was a bad experience for her. I understood the problem, because I knew him, and he was a dickhead. I heard he told her that he didn't like women telling him what to do. Lorraine was a highly competent and skilled police officer with a bit of an edge. I respected her. She was tough on me, in the beginning anyway. I had to earn her trust. At that time, during field training the trainee was evaluated in many categories such as uniform, promptness, knowledge of the paperwork, etc. The highest score possible was a 7, and those were rare. I learned a lot from Lorraine, and even after field training was over, I would still seek her advice on certain reports. We became friends, and I always enjoyed working with her.

During my training with Lorraine, we responded to a domestic dispute. The dispatcher reported someone had called 911 and a lot of yelling could be heard in the background. Someone was stabbed and bleeding, they informed us, and all parties involved were still at the scene. We arrived to a large number of people on the front lawn of the residence. There was what looked like a kitchen knife on the ground in the grass. Lorraine moved quickly and ordered me to move people back as she secured the knife. We learned quickly that mommy and daughter were sleeping with the same guy. Needless to say, not every neighborhood on Long Island is idyllic and family friendly.

The daughter was handcuffed and Lorraine asked me to watch her while she addressed the mother. I was watching her and trying to keep onlookers at bay. I suddenly noticed the daughter had slipped out of the handcuffs. This is not uncommon with petite women; they tried to handcuff me in the Academy during a tactical training drill and I easily slipped out of them. I yelled to Lorraine to look out as the daughter lunged at her, and I tackled the daughter to the ground.

Rookies would be called in by a Sergeant or Lieutenant to go over the previous week's training assessments, and to my happy surprise, Lorraine had given me a 7 for 'use of force.' I smiled to myself.

After a few weeks with Lorraine, my next Field Training Officer was Joe, who had a different style of training. He was more low key and was very patient with me. Joe also worked in the middle class neighborhood of Commack, whereas Lorraine worked in the rougher part of town. Joe taught me to be more personable, as I was a bit stoic.

If the bosses felt you were ready and had a good grasp of what you were doing they would end your field training at 10 weeks instead of the 12 weeks. I was doing well, learning a lot and enjoying the experience, so I wasn't looking to get my field training cut short. But the bosses said I was ready, and cut my training with a field trainer at 10 weeks. I could learn whatever else I needed through on the job experience.

The first year out of the Academy you were on probation, which meant if you screwed up on or off duty, you could be fired without cause or reason. During that period I would not do much of anything with friends. I worked. I slept. Wash, rinse, repeat. I well knew at that time no one really loved the idea of a female cop on the force, and I did not want to give them any possible reason to let me go. Once you completed that probationary period and all the necessary requirements, and did not get yourself into trouble, you were covered, and the department would need 'just cause' to terminate you. When I completed my probationary period, I felt a weight had been lifted off my shoulders. I took a deep cleansing breath, and relaxed a little. It took a while for it to sink in. I had made it. I was a police officer. Not just a wannabe mall cop. Now, when I put on the uniform, it was me—not just an aspiration.

Something had become apparent during my first year as a cop. Right after the small class that followed us in the Academy, a hiring freeze was put into place. That meant I would be low man on the totem pole until more cops were hired. I was one of the last to pick vacation days. Oh yeah, February vacation, here I come! As it turned out, they would not hire for another seven years—and I was low man for all that time.

When you begin your duties as a police officer on your own, you start as a relief driver—if someone calls in sick, they fill the car with you. Everything was governed by seniority, and I had none, so I did what I was told to do and went where I was told to go. I was the newbie, and I just sucked it up and did whatever was asked of me. As a relief driver, I had to call the precinct each day and asked where in the precinct I would be assigned. It was an unsettling way to live. Every day I bounced, unless I was fortunate enough to get the same sector car for a week while the regular operator was on vacation, or at the Academy for training. I did good work and the bosses appreciated me for it; maybe even liked me for not giving them grief as others did. So I was plenty surprised when a steady sector car became available in an area I knew well, and I was offered the car. I was excited to say the least. However, one of the male cops who was, how do I put this, a low performance sissy boy, started whining that he had more seniority than me and he should be given the car regardless of his lackluster performance. Seniority is king, and the bosses eventually folded.

It was around this time when things with Ray started winding down in earnest. I had a new love, my job, and as for Ray, he may have met someone new also. I had left the quaint apartment to live with Ray, but I needed to find my own place. I did not want to rent, so I began to look for houses closer to work, but most of those houses were out of my financial reach. I was a North Shore girl and Smithtown was just right for me. I worked there and new the neighborhoods well.

There was an exclusive part of Smithtown known as the Smithtown Pines. The houses were expensive there, but I found a house that was in foreclosure, and I wondered what was up with the sale. It turned out a lawyer ended up with it and was looking to flip it for a big profit, even though he had not put the necessary work in to justify the price. It was in pretty bad shape, cosmetically, anyway. I put in a bid offering $100,000 less than his asking price. He just laughed at me and politely asked me to leave. I waited patiently and let him eat it for a few weeks. I called him again and asked, "How are those mortgage payments going for you? Got a buyer yet?"

"Okay, let's talk," he said.

After some back and forth, we came to an agreed upon price—very close to my number, not his; much to his dismay. Still, what I paid for the house was a lot of money for a single woman in the year 2000, and especially on a police officer's salary.

I moved into my home in the spring of 2000. It was close to the 4th Precinct. Buying this house was the fulfillment of the American dream for me. I was patriotic and appreciated the unique personal liberty afforded to me and everyone else by the underlying principles of America. The first thing I did was buy an American flag and put it up in the front of the house. My mother came over with family to see my new home. She got out of the car and saw the flag and pointed to it and said, "What the fuck is that?"

"What is what?" I was perplexed

"That!" she pointed accusingly at the flag.

Now, I understood my mother had worked for the state and constantly depended on government assistance when I was young—and she was a taker, politically speaking. I decided to go easy on her and not chastise her for her anti American ignorance. That's an American flag, I said respectfully. It's the symbol of our country, where we are free to build our lives. I am living the American dream, and I'm grateful for the opportunity this free nation provides to me—so I have an American flag in front of my house.

She looked at the flag, then at me. She turned to walk toward the door and said, "That's fucking ridiculous."

I had no furniture to speak of—a small sofa, a chair and a mattress. I had always lived with someone else in a house; my family, a boyfriend or my landlady. This was the first time I was totally alone in a house—it was a bit scary, and liberating at the same time. At first I set up my mattress on the hardwood floor in the living room. I slept in the long, vacant room; just a girl and her gun. The house was a ranch style single story with an unfinished, bare bones huge basement.

The house needed a lot of work. The airy gap under the front door provided a nice breeze in May, but in October it had to be remedied. I found yard work to be cathartic, and it provided a lot of exercise, so I spent a lot of time doing my own landscaping. The house had a nice circular driveway, but no garage.

The first year I owned the house I worked over 800 hours of overtime to be able to afford a new roof, new front door, and new windows. Over the next 10 years I would slowly continue to upgrade the house, doing many of the repairs myself.

It was my life, and would be the foundation of my eventual retirement. It was the American dream, and I was living it. I knew a family would be purchasing the home from me when I left, so all of the upgrades and remodeling were completed with the needs and tastes of a family in mind. It was my home for the next 17 years, and I loved it.

⬥ ⬥ ⬥

Being a 'small in stature' police officer usually worked against me. One time, it saved a life. I was a relief driver working the east side of the precinct when I received a radio call that a man claiming to be an attorney called in a welfare check on a possibly suicidal client. I went over to the house and knocked on the door, but there was no answer. I walked around the front and sides of the house, looking in the windows and checking the doors. All locked. I walked up to the garage, and I heard an engine running inside.

"Oh shit." Just then a second patrol car pulled up. I looked in the car and recognized him as an officer I knew well. "Look, there's a woman inside, and I just checked and there's no way inside other than through the garage door. I think she's got the car running in the garage." He knew what that meant. The only way was in through the small garage door windows. He looked at them then at me.

"I can make it—help me," I said. He found a brick and broke out the window. It took out the entire window. He helped me up and I barely squeezed through.

I hurried to the car and saw the woman in the driver's seat. I just prayed that she hadn't locked the door. The fumes were heavy and I was already choking, gasping for oxygen. I knew a very heavy woman like her wouldn't last very long, so I threw open the door and leaned across her to turn the car off and take away the keys.

I rushed to the side of the garage door and found the button to open it, and the motor kicked in and started the noisy grind of lifting the heavy door. The male cop came inside and walked over to the open car door and looked in, and I said, "I wouldn't get too close if I were you. I don't think she's really that friendly to men just now."

The woman stirred, and saw him there and started thrashing around, and he backed out quickly. I walked over and started soothing her—"Yeah, I know that men can be fucking pigs when they wanna be." That got her attention, and she immediately began to calm down.

My Sergeant was clear he didn't like female cops, but he put me in for a lifesaving award. The committee that decides who gets the award (sitting behind a desk) denied it, saying I was not injured enough to merit the award. Bullshit. Even my Sergeant was pissed at them.

* * *

September 11, 2001 — 07:24

Four Islamic terrorists, members of al-Qaida, checked in at the United Airlines desk for their morning flight from Newark International Airport in New Jersey to San Francisco International Airport in California. Checking in for Flight 93 were Ahmed al-Nami, Ahmed al-Haznawi, Saeed al-Ghamdi and Ziad Jarrah, the most recent recruit to Islamic Extremism. Ghamdi and Nami arrived at the counter first, just after 7:00 a.m. Haznawi arrived at 7:24. Jarrah was on the public telephone with his girlfriend, Aysel Sengün, repeating the words, "I love you," over and over. Jarrah's habit of clinging too tightly to his family and girlfriend kept him under close al-Qaida scrutiny, but another potential member of the team had been intercepted and returned to the Middle East—so there was no one else available for the hijacking. As it was, the team had only four members, while the other three hijacking teams had five each.

Haznawi and Ghamdi walked down the jetway and boarded the plane at 7:39, taking their places in first class seats 6B and 3D. Nami boarded one minute later and sat in first class seat 3C. Ziad Jarrah finally hung up the phone and boarded the aircraft at 7:48 sitting in seat 1B. Flight 93 had 33 regular passengers, plus the four terrorists, and seven crew members—only 20 percent filled. The crew members were Captain Jason Dahl and First Officer LeRoy Homer, Jr., and flight attendants Lorraine Bay, Sandra Bradshaw, Wanda Green, CeeCee Lyles and Deborah Welsh.

The plane pushed back from gate A17 on time at 8:01 a.m., but heavy airport traffic kept it on the tarmac for 40 minutes. The four terrorists were very nervous about the long delay, because they knew that Flight 11 would be hitting the World Trade Center North Tower in just a few minutes, robbing them of the element of surprise, and possibly causing all flights still on the tarmac to be grounded. Flight 93 finally lifted off at 8:42 a.m., and quickly reached its cruising altitude of 35,000 feet, even while Flight 11 was crashing into the North Tower.

As the news of airplane hijackings began to spread, air traffic officials began issuing warnings through the Aircraft Communication Addressing and Reporting System (ACARS). Ed Ballinger, the United Airlines flight dispatcher, sent text warnings to United Airlines flights at 9:19. At 9:22, First Officer LeRoy Homer's wife, Melody, had an ACARS message sent to her husband in the cockpit asking if he was all right. Two minutes later Flight 93 received Ballinger's ACARS warning, "Beware any cockpit intrusion – two a/c hit World Trade Center."

At 9:26 a.m. Captain Jason Dahl sent an ACARS message back saying, "Ed, confirm latest mssg plz —Jason."

Two minutes later the terrorists broke into the cockpit and attacked the pilots, and the aircraft dropped 680 feet in just thirty seconds during the scuffle. The Cleveland controller and other pilots flying in the vicinity heard unintelligible sounds of screaming and fighting. A Cleveland Air Traffic Controller radioed and asked, "Somebody call Cleveland?" There was no immediate reply, but 35 seconds later Flight 93 made another transmission, and First Officer LeRoy Homer shouted, "Mayday! Mayday! Get out of here! Get out of here! Get out of here!"

Ziad Jarrah, who had trained as a pilot, took control of the aircraft and pulled it out of its dive, and turned it back in the direction of Washington, D.C., and the terrorists' target, the U.S. Capitol Building. Captain Dahl was still in the pilot's seat, unconscious for a time, and Jarrah turned on the auto pilot.

* * *

September 11, 2001 — 08:40

While air traffic controllers were fixated on American Airlines Flight 11 heading back toward New York City, United Flight 175's transponder signal changed twice within a minute, and the aircraft began deviating from its course. It was four minutes before the air traffic controller in charge of Flight 175 noticed the inconsistencies of the flight. Flight 175 was changing altitude and the controller jumped on the radio and made five unsuccessful attempts to contact the flight crew.

Flight attendant Robert Fangman got on the GTE airphones in the rear of the plane and called the United Airlines maintenance office in San Francisco and spoke with Marc Policastro. He reported the hijacking and said the pilots were dead and the hijackers were flying the plane. He also said that a flight attendant had been stabbed. The call was cut off, and Policastro tried to contact the plane's cockpit using the ACARS message system, writing, "I heard of a reported incident aboard your acft. Plz verify all is normal." No answer came.

Brian David Sweeney tried calling his wife, Julie, at 8:58, but she didn't answer. He left a ended u message saying their plane had been hijacked. He then called his parents and spoke with his mother, Louise, telling her they had been hijacked and said, "Some passengers are considering storming the cockpit and taking back control of the plane." Sweeney told her the hijackers were coming back, and said "goodbye," and hung up.

At 8:52, Peter Hanson called his father, Lee Hanson, in Easton, Connecticut. He whispered into the phone, telling him their plane had been hijacked and the pilots were dead, and a flight attendant had been stabbed. He said the terrorists were flying really erratically, and he was especially upset because he was traveling with his wife, Sue, and their two-year-old daughter, Christine. Hanson asked his father to contact United Airlines and tell them what was happening, but Lee couldn't get through to them, so he called the local police.

At 8:58 a.m. the flight was over New Jersey at 28,500 feet, and as Shehhi completed the final turn back toward Manhattan he put the plane into a power dive, descending 24,000 feet in just five minutes. Delta Air Lines Flight 2315 was flying from Hartford to Tampa, and saw the diving plane at the last second, and they nearly collided, missing each other by a mere 100 yards.

Peter Hanson made a second phone call to his father at 9:00. "It's getting bad, Dad. A stewardess was stabbed. They seem to have knives and mace. They said they have a bomb. It's getting very bad on the plane. Passengers are throwing up and getting sick. The plane is making jerky movements. I don't think the pilot is flying the plane. I think we are going down. I think they intend to go to Chicago or someplace and fly into a building. Don't worry, Dad. If it happens, it'll be very fast ... Oh my God ... oh my God, oh my God." The call ended as Hanson's father heard a woman screaming in the airplane.

Air traffic controller Dave Bottiglia was frantic, yelling at pilots passing Flight 175, "Take any evasive action necessary! We have an airplane that we don't know what he's doing. Any action at all." Within moments Flight 175 nearly collided with Midwest Express Flight 7 as well, as they made their way from Milwaukee to New York.

Marwan al-Shehhi brought the plane in fast at 590 m.p.h. and had to bank hard to get a direct hit on the South Tower. As the plane leaned to the left the passengers could see the smoke and flames rising from the North Tower of the World

Trade Center where American Airlines Flight 11 had exploded just 17 minutes earlier. Flight 175 slammed into the southern façade of the South Tower at one second before 9:03 a.m., entering between floors 77 and 85. The 10,000 gallons of jet fuel erupted into a fiery explosion, instantly killing everyone on board, plus hundreds more in the South Tower.

One of the three stairwells in the South Tower was still intact after the impact, but only 18 people were able to pass the impact zone through the stairway and get out of the South Tower before it collapsed. Some of those above the point of impact made their way upward trying to get to the roof where a helicopter could rescue them. The access doors to the roof were locked, however, and the intense heat and smoke prevented helicopters from landing on the roof.

The South Tower burned for 56 minutes before collapsing and killing over 600 people.

Chapter 7 — Life and Death

A woman's body was wheeled in and I looked at her. I had seen dead bodies before, many times now in the Ground Zero morgue. She was so covered with ash that she seemed just a little bit make believe—maybe like a movie prop or a wax museum character. Of course, this comprehension was just part of my coping mechanism. Beneath the thick ash I could see that she was a fairly young woman, maybe in her thirties, with long dark hair and white features. I could see serious burning and other damage to parts of her face and body. She had a purse at her side, and a shoulder strap that came across her body and over her shoulder. I could tell that the strap and bag had been exposed to extreme heat and the strap was essentially seared to her clothing and body. The smell that attended the burn victims was disturbing to me at first, no matter how I tried to get the smell out, I could not. It would linger in the air, and on my clothes and in my nose long after the body was removed. The smell of burning charred flesh is not something you soon forget.

I'd glove up in preparation for the unpleasant task of trying to find identification on her person. I carefully opened the bag trying not to touch any of the metal parts because they were still super-heated and I could easily burn myself if I wasn't careful. I was able to open the bag enough though and found that the heat had pretty much sealed everything together inside. I was able to retrieve her driver's license and was surprised that it was not only intact, but quite legible. I held the license up to the light hanging above the examination table and slowly read the name, then spelled it out for the officer documenting the information on the stool in the corner. Her name, her date of birth, her address, height and weight. These were the sum of a person—for the purposes of establishing identification, in that sad setting anyway.

I learned fast that whereas most dead bodies begin to cool as soon as they expire, some of the bodies brought into us from the Pile had lain in smoldering materials since the attack, and were heated far beyond normal body temperature. I had to be careful when I was required to touch a body that I did not touch metal straps or buckles. The bodies were very warm to the touch, and I had to constantly remind myself that they were not alive, and that they were beyond medical assistance.

My emotional journey during the process would usually take a fork in the road at the point where the lifeless body on the table would now have a photograph on the I.D. depicting the person in full life—in living color, as it were. At that moment where I could now picture the person alive, smiling, with a name—this is the point where my cop detachment would be challenged by my humanity, and a great sense of human loss would wash over me. This was a person. A person with feelings, fears, friends and family, and experiences. These were our neighbors. Now, the body was still, covered in a coat of gray ash and badly singed from the searing heat.

The Examiner would then examine the remains to be sure that the identification recovered with the body could be the same lifeless body that had possessed that identification. When the M.E. was finished with his examination, and everything that needed to be recorded and documented was completed, the remains and any items brought in with the body were readied for transport.

Remains would leave the temporary morgue and be escorted over to the New York City Examiner's Office building on 26th Street, where items were meticulously catalogued, and additional, more detailed examinations would be performed. DNA and data would be entered. Their preliminary I.D. that we had conducted would be used as a starting point in that more thorough examination. Requests for personal items such as toothbrushes and hairbrushes belonging to the victims were made by the Medical Examiner's office to loved ones. Those items would be taken into the M.E.'s office, and DNA pulled from them could be used to match DNA obtained from the actual bodies recovered. DNA identification and matching was not as advanced in 2001 as it is today. As of this writing, experts are still working to identify some remains of victims of the World Trade Center terror attack.

For the purposes of preliminary identification, the process was simpler in the beginning as intact bodies would be brought in. It became more difficult as whole bodies gave way to parts and pieces found in the rubble. Responders were sifting through tons and tons of twisted steel and reinforced concrete desperately searching, in the beginning at least, for the living. When all hope of survival had faded the maneuvers became recovery operations. Bodies were recovered. Then limbs and torsos. Then tiny bits of flesh, and fragments of bone. The workers were weary, even the cadaver dogs began to show signs of fatigue. It was almost a relief at times when we would get a small piece of flesh that a cadaver dog had located that would turn out to be a piece of chicken, that presumably had come from the Windows on the World restaurant at the top of the North Tower. Even these items would be sent to the Examiner's building for confirmation.

■ ■ ■

On the warm summer evening of July 17, 1996, TWA Flight 800 sat on the runway of JFK Airport headed for Rome, Italy, with a stopover in Paris, France. It was a Boeing 747-131 jumbo jetliner filled with 230 people, 212 passengers and 18 crew, originating from over 30 countries. There were families headed for famous vacation hotspots, and students who were fortunate enough to visit the bright lights and galleries of the famed cities of Europe. Excitement was in the air as dreams were coming true for so many passengers. At 8:19 p.m. the captain released the brakes and the airliner started out, then began to rapidly pick up speed and within a moment lifted from the runway and headed east over Long Island's Great South Bay toward the Atlantic Ocean. Dusk had just fallen over the land and as the lights of the plane gained altitude, it attracted the interest of hundreds on the ground, watching and wondering where the passengers might be headed on their overnight flight east.

Within 12 minutes of takeoff TWA 800 reached 13,000 feet as it approached the city of East Moriches, about two-thirds of the way across the length of Long Island. Observers from the towns, beaches, backyards and boats below noticed a small white flame trailing the flight, and then it suddenly exploded, sending the gigantic fireball to the water below in large sections. Witnesses watched in horror as they realized that everyone aboard the commercial passenger jet had just died together, within a single heartbeat. It was obvious that no one could have survived that horrific firestorm in the sky.

That night thousands of first responders and volunteers, together with hundreds from the media and general rubberneckers poured into Suffolk County, adding to the mass chaos that existed from the downed commercial flight. I was called into work at the 4th Precinct and told, "You're ready— you're off training early—we need you." That was it. My first solo assignment would now be assisting in the TWA Flight #800 disaster.

At that time the 4th Precinct shared a parking lot with the Suffolk County Medical Examiner's Crime Lab. It was one of the premier medical examiners offices and lab facilities in the nation.

When you were hired by the Police Department, they would ask you about your previous experience and skills. My Lieutenant knew of my past training with disasters, more specifically, exercises involving plane disaster scenarios when I had worked for the Red Cross. I was assigned to the medical examiner's office where they knew they could use my experience and because I was the rookie, and no other cop liked sitting behind a desk.

Tensions were very high as the bodies began to be brought to the Medical Examiner's Office, because no one yet knew the cause of the passenger jet's demise. The U.S. had already been on high alert due to threats coming out of the Middle East, and Iran and Libya were high on the suspect list. The eyewitnesses had nearly unanimously reported a small trail of fire in the sky leading to the commercial jet just as it exploded, which pointed to the possibility of a surface to air missile. There was widespread fear of all sorts of unconfirmed reports of missiles and additional bombings, and threats of additional acts of terror were being called into local authorities and local media. The National Transportation Safety Board (NTSB) was investigating every possible theory at the time.

We were on high alert at the M.E.'s offices, which had tended to draw a lot of unwanted attention as the place where all of the bodies and their belongings were being transported. I was a cop, with a badge and a gun, and it was my job to protect the facilities, the workers and the visitors. It was hard, because there was often something of a circus atmosphere, with the media sneaking around trying to get shots of dead bodies and grieving loved ones, and we who were trying to provide security never knowing who was legitimate and who might be there for nefarious purposes. Members of the media were trying every artifice to creep onto the grounds, even pretending to be grieving family of the deceased to gain access with their hidden cameras.

Many bodies a day were coming in, and they were in various states of decomposition. One body arrived and I checked for identification, and found his passport in his shirt breast pocket. His passport was in surprisingly good condition, and we could see his photograph clearly, and read the details about him. He was a British citizen, like many of the passengers, and a police officer. Flight 800 included a class of school children who were going to France.

I had to deal with a number of remains while working with the M.E.'s office. That didn't bother me as much as I thought it might. What bothered me the most was when I began to see the photographs of the dead, in their normal lives. There was a large, empty wall in the back of the facility, and the M.E. began to put photographs of the victims up on the wall, as something of a memorial, I guess. Family members had been dropping them off for a few weeks, and they were accumulating in drawers, so one day the M.E. began taping them to the wall, then had the staff continue doing it. Seeing them with their loved ones, smiling and living their lives— that was the hard part for me. As lifeless victims of a disaster, I was able to detach myself from the reality of their deaths somewhat. But seeing them happy and full of life, that changed things for me.

One of the victims in a photograph had a parrot on his shoulder—and looked so exuberant. One young woman in her early thirties looked so vibrant, and her friends told me that she always talked about living to be 100, because that was the only way she'd be able to experience everything about life on her list. That really resonated with me. There were hundreds who were taken long before their time, and I felt the weight of that loss. It was at that point that my daily drives home became tearful as I looked for a way to release the anguish I felt for the dead. I never had to deal with the remains of any of the children during my months working on TWA 800. I thanked God for that every day. It would have been too much for me, I'm sure.

I was often assigned to the front desk in the foyer of the Examiner's Office. A desk with folding chairs had been set up for the police officers that were assigned there to help control the volume of people coming in. Nearly all of the TWA Flight 800 victims were taken to the Suffolk County Medical Examiner's Office, and in addition to this disaster, there was the regular volume of cases coming in. The office staff was overwhelmed. Funeral homes were picking up remains, and many of the visitors were family and close friends of the deceased coming in to ask for information, identify remains or pick up belongings.

As a newly activated police officer, I was temporarily assigned to the M.E.'s Office and given a fairly regular schedule; usually working 12 to 16 hour days, Monday through Saturday. One morning they requested me to drive the Medical Examiner from his office in Hauppauge to Moriches, near the wreckage site. I went in early to ensure the patrol vehicle was clean and filled up with gas to make sure it was a pleasant experience for the M.E., who was truly serving at an elevated level. After picking the M.E. up at his office we headed out to Moriches—he was extremely bright and intense, and a great conversationalist. He was amused by my story about "Quincy, M.E.," and my high school aspirations to become a medical examiner. He was taken with me, and requested from the department that I be reassigned from the front desk to the back where I could help him and his staff directly.

The M.E. was no fan of the press. I once saw him walking down the hall with the small paper bin over his head saying, "I hate the media! I hate the media!" I laughed and walked with him to make sure he wasn't assailed by any more wayward press personnel. After that, I made it my mission to ensure the media was kept at Bay, because other than regular press briefings, there was no legitimate reason for them to be there. The media tried every dirty little trick to get in—I heard that one night they had even tried dressing up as clergy to get in. Fucking ghouls.

I was asked to escort the M.E. to the crash site again, and to the hangar where the commercial airliner was being reconstructed. Very few were afforded that privilege. Those who did the reconstruction did a phenomenal job getting everything back into place like a giant metal puzzle. The jet had gone down in water, so to collect all the pieces and put it back together was a herculean task. As I studied the plane I could see how the metal skin was blasted outward, flowering out, evidencing an explosion from the inside of the plane. I wasn't sure, but it seemed like strong evidence to me that the explosion was not a missile attack. But I'm no expert— perhaps a missile enters the fuselage, then explodes. I was dubious. Word was that it was compressed gas tanks that exploded—like oxygen. A damned shame—but most likely, in my mind.

As I walked with my escort through the facility, I saw two pieces of metal from the interior of the aircraft that had been joined together with duct tape at the factory. I smiled a little to myself and the thought occurred to me that a photo of these two pieces duct taped together following such a notorious explosion and plummet to earth would make a great commercial for the product. 'Is there anything duct tape can't do?'

Some of the medical people working on TWA Flight 800 operations told me that they were members of the volunteer organization Disaster Mortuary Operations Response Team (D.M.O.R.T.), and suggested that they could really use a police officer with disaster training and experience on the team. D.M.O.R.T. responds to emergencies throughout the region and the nation, and members travel throughout the United States to gain unique training from experts around the country. They are first responders in times of disaster, and give medical and other aid, helping with recovery, etc. It was run under federal Health and Human Services (before Homeland Security.) The TWA Flight 800 disaster had proved to me that disasters really happen, and that someone should be trained to know what to do then the unthinkable happens. I joined D.M.O.R.T., and went for the training. They issued my equipment and uniform, and I waited for my first activation. They taught us everything we needed to know in the event of a disaster, and I had my equipment and go-bag ready to go. We were assigned teams, and I was given instructions where to show up if the shit hit the fan.

■ ■ ■

September 11, 2001 — 09:30

The Flight 93 hijackers quickly moved the passengers and flight attendants to the rear of the plane and Jarrah tried to announce over the system, but broadcast to the air controllers, "Ladies and gentlemen: here the captain. Please sit down, keep remaining seating. We have a bomb on board. So sit."

During the broadcast, air controllers heard first-class flight attendant Debbie Welsh struggling in the background, saying, "Please, please, don't hurt me."

The air traffic controller understood the transmission, and was anxious for the flight attendant, but responded, "Calling Cleveland Center, you're unreadable. Say again, slowly."

Jarrah took the aircraft up to 40,700 feet, and air traffic controllers went to work clearing several aircraft out of the new flightpath.

Debbie Welsh pleaded again, "I don't want to die, I don't want to die," and then went silent.

One of the hijackers immediately said in Arabic, *"Everything is fine. I finished."*

At 9:39, just two minutes after Flight 77 impacted the Pentagon, air traffic controllers overheard Jarrah say, "Ah, here's the captain. I would like you all to remain seated. We have a bomb aboard, and we are going back to the airport, and we have our demands. So please remain quiet."

The passengers and crew began making phone calls to family members and airline officials around 9:30 a.m., using onboard phones and personal cell phones. Altogether, 10 passengers and two crew members were able to connect with their calls, informing family, friends and others on the ground what was happening to them.

Tom Burnett made several phone calls to his wife, telling her that the plane had been hijacked by men claiming to have a bomb. He also said a passenger had been stabbed with a knife and that he believed the bomb threat was only a ruse, to control the passengers. During one of his calls, his wife told him about the attacks on the World Trade Center. "The hijackers were talking about crashing this plane. ... Oh my God," he realized, "it's a suicide mission." He asked his wife for details about the WTC attacks, and kept interrupting her to tell others nearby what she was reporting. He ended his last call telling her, "Don't worry. We're going to do something."

Flight attendant Sandra Bradshaw called the United maintenance facility at 09:35, reporting the flight had been hijacked, "by men with knives who were in the cabin and flight deck, and stabbed another flight attendant, possibly Debbie Welsh."

Mark Bingham called his mother at 9:37 and told her that the plane had been hijacked by three men who claimed to have a bomb.

The passengers on Flight 93 were hearing from their family and friends that Flight 77 had hit the Pentagon, and Flights 11 and 175 had struck the World Trade Center Twin Towers. They discussed among themselves the probability that their own hijacked aircraft was destined for an equally strategic target, and asked for ideas what they could do to stop the terrorists from succeeding in their evil mission.

Jeremy Glick called his wife and explained that their flight had been hijacked "by three dark-skinned men who look Iranian." He said they wore red bandanas and had knives. He was able to stay on the line with her for the remainder of the flight. He told her that the passengers had voted whether they should rush the terrorists, and they were going to do something soon.

Joseph DeLuca called his father at 9:43 and told him what was happening. Todd Beamer tried to call his wife at the same time, but was routed to GTE phone operator Lisa Jefferson. He told her the flight had been hijacked and that two people who he thought were the pilots were on the floor in the front of the plane, and were probably dead. He reported that one of the hijackers had a red belt with what looked like a bomb strapped to his waist.

Captain Jason Dahl revived and struggled with Ziad Jarrah, trying to wrest control of the plane from him, interfering with the auto pilot, continuing to turn it off while Jarrah fought to keep it engaged. Jarrah suddenly pulled the plane a hard bank south, and Todd Beamer told his wife, "We're going down! We're going down!"

"*This green knob?*" a hijacker asked in Arabic.

"Yes, that's the one," Jarrah confirmed.

At 9:41 Captain Dahl moaned, and said, "Oh, man!"

One of the hijackers said, "Inform them, and tell him to talk to the pilot; bring the pilot back," probably referring to Homer, lying semi-conscious outside of the cockpit.

Linda Gronlund called her sister, Elsa Strong, at 9:46, leaving the message—"There are men with a bomb." Flight attendant CeeCee Lyles was able to leave a phone message with her husband telling him they had been hijacked.

Marion Britton called her friend, Fred Fiumano, at 09:49, telling him, "We're gonna—they're gonna kill us, you know. We're gonna die."

Fred Fiumano didn't know what to say to her. He saw on his television what had happened at the World Trade Center, but he just told her, "Don't worry, they hijacked the plane, and they're gonna take you for a ride. You go to their country, and you come back. You stay there for vacation." As she continued to cry and scream, he repeated, "Be calm. Just stay calm. You'll be all right."

Flight attendant Sandra Bradshaw called her husband and told him she was heating up water to throw at the hijackers. "Everyone is running up to first class. I've got to go. Bye."

Chapter 8 — In Our Genes

The M.E. was very knowledgeable and impressed me almost nightly. On one occasion, individual bones were brought into the temporary morgue. The M.E. studied them as he put on a fresh pair of gloves. He picked up a long bone that even I recognized as a femur. He examined it, paying close attention to the femoral head, then lifting it up gently he looked at the femoral neck. Unfortunately, we received a lot of bare bones, because the extreme heat and impact ended up stripping away most of the soft tissues. I watched him closely, wondering if he would be able to tell us anything at all about who it had belonged to.

As the M.E. continued to study the bone, I could not help but notice how clean it was, and aside from its gray color, it looked like a model bone for a medical class. The M.E. looked at me, and signaled for me to come stand next to him. "This femur belonged to a black male, approximately 30 years old, and you see right here," he pointed to the femoral head of the bone, "he was developing arthritis."

He glanced over at me, noticing the questioning look on my face. In fact, I was wondering how the hell he knew all of that. "Okay, most of the human races are different in some ways from the other races." I was not sure where he was going with this but it sounded logical, so I listened. "See how this part of the femur comes to a point in the front?" He angled the bone so I could see what he was talking about. I looked and nodded. "Black males have longer and higher bone density than white males of a similar age. Some tend to think the femur is more aerodynamic than that of a white male because of these factors. Based on these findings and studies still to be done, we can tell the difference between age, race, gender, health and other factors."

Damn. Color me impressed.

The purpose of a preliminary identification, and to the extent the M.E.'s expertise was brought to bear, was these types of observations. Inevitably, this did help match missing persons with DNA samples provided by loved ones, in that the search could be narrowed when these parameters were entered into the database. Our efforts to narrow down the search helped bring faster closure to families and friends waiting to find out what had happened to their loved ones.

Throughout my time working on the Pile, the M.E. often showed me other bones and pointed out shape, size, chips and deep wear marks from tendons or muscles and explained what may have caused those characteristics and whose bone it may have been as a result. I watched as he would present his case with care and the usual detached interest of a scholar, and realized that his pragmatic attitude had probably developed as his medical school professors had assigned him and his classmates months of cadaver dissection and study. I had heard that this was extremely difficult for the first few days, but got easier as weeks passed. I had seen death and mayhem on the job, and during TWA Flight 800. I wasn't ever going to get used to this though. Every scene was different for me. He was a full time medical examiner, and had long ago gotten used to dead bodies. In the moment, I envied him. In the long term, I did not.

The slow nights were the worst nights. With not much for me to do, I spent too much time thinking. My head was spinning. It was the constant attack on my senses. You would think the down time would be good for me, but in actuality it only made things much worse. I would stare blankly into the great abyss that used to be the New York City skyline. Smoldering ash would rise and fall with a backdrop of high powered spotlights creating shadows of death and destruction as far as I could see. All I could hear were cranes and other heavy machinery being used to remove the rubble.

Where the towers once stood and the surrounding streets had now become an enclosed micro city within New York City, all encircled with cement barriers to keep most people out, and others in. One of the access points was dedicated to large trucks and vehicles carting off the twisted steel and cement. Crushed vehicles that had been parked on the streets below were now stacked on the back of maxi trailers that strained to pull their load.

Much of the debris that was hauled from the Pile was taken to the Fresh Kills Landfill on Staten Island where it would be separated, sorted and searched again. To some, this may sound cold and disrespectful, but there was literally no space to remove debris anywhere else that had the land and the facilities open to support such a monumental task.

It was about two weeks into my work on the Pile that letters started arriving from all around the U.S. These letters were mostly from grade school children, written in a child's clumsy handwriting; some with crayon then some with pencil or pen, but all had the same message—that they were sad for us and thanked us. These letters were handed out to us by volunteers. I have read every one of them that I received, and I still have them all, and read them all on every anniversary.

The Joe DiMaggio Highway, more commonly known as the West Highway, runs from West 72nd Street along the Hudson River to the southernmost point of Manhattan. This was the main entry point for many first responders. This was also where many would gather; citizens who did not flee the city on the days following the attacks. They would come and line the West Highway with signs thanking first responders and flying American flags. Others had come to donate goods like bottled water, gloves, hats and boots. The West Side Highway became known as "thank you" highway, and a temporary sign was erected to convey that message.

I worked nights and we did not arrive to much fanfare. We did the work no one wanted to talk about, much less think about. The messy part of life—dying, and what happens to the body after death, especially when that death was sudden and violent.

* * *

My ex-boyfriend called. "I heard you're working on the Pile." He sounded surprised. Figures.

"Yes, I am. I'm working with D.M.O.R.T. in a secure area next to the Pile," I said, trying not to sound annoyed.

"Wow, I'm surprised YOU are working there," he quipped. He sounded pretty condescending. Yep, that was why he was my ex. That conversation reminded me why I gave him the exit interview—there was only room for one little girl in that relationship, notwithstanding I had long ago put on my big girl panties.

I bumped into him a few years later and he told me he had cancer, and they had caught it early. I was very aware that many of those who had worked on the Pile were developing cancer, so I asked if he had spoken to someone at the World Trade Center Program or met with an attorney who specialized in WTC cases. He had not. I suggested who he should call and what to do. I even gave him my attorney's number. My help resulted in a hefty payout, and I jokingly asked if there would be a finder's fee. He bluntly said no.

Wow—not even dinner.

* * *

After a few years as a relief driver, I was asked to work the desk in the 4th Precinct on a steady basis. I had a Lieutenant at the time who was also an attorney. He was a micro manager, and not well liked. Although he was bright, many felt he was too smart for his own good. He knew I was respectful and would not give him a hard time. He was also well aware that my paperwork was organized and that I was efficient. I liked working the desk. There was always something going on; phones ringing, people coming in to ask questions or to file a police report. There was always something to do. I also liked being around other people, unlike working solo in a sector car.

The precinct was located in Smithtown and my house was nearby. I worked the desk with two other police officers, Mike and Bobby, two great cops, who worked well together but could not have been more opposite in their personalities. Bobby was the humorous one, and Mike was the calm, unflappable one. They were patient with me and taught me a great deal and I could always rely on them if I was unsure about a report or procedure.

The 4th Precinct served as the women's detention facility for the county. This meant every female prisoner that could not get to court that day for any reason and had to be held overnight must be taken to the 4th Precinct. Other precincts would be required to drop off their female prisoners along with any and all documents required by the courts. Usually, it was the duty of the desk Sergeant or Lieutenant to ensure that all documents were in order. My Lieutenant would tell the cops bringing in female prisoners, "You go up to the front desk and show Stacey your paperwork, and anything she says for you to do is like an order coming from me." Now, a supervisor who delegates is great in my view, and I appreciated his trust in me—but it often put me in an awkward position with the other cops. Sometimes a senior guy would get a bit annoyed with me when I told him he needed to redo some of his paperwork. Most of the time it was an easy fix, but they all got pissed and let me know it. I had a good rapport with most of the officers and some of the staff that were responsible for collecting the paperwork. I knew what they needed, and often there would be slight requirement changes that the courts would make, and I was sure to keep up on all those changes so it would be easier on the guys doing the paperwork. You're welcome!

Although I had abandoned my acting career, I found that many of my stage skills translated well to dealing with the press. I was young and cute, and looked pretty damn good in uniform! Patrol cops were not normally allowed to speak to the media unless directed to do so by a supervisor. Most inquiries from the public or the media went through the Suffolk County Public Information Office, and this office was also responsible for all press releases. Most cops did not like dealing directly with the media. I not only didn't mind, I liked it, and I used each opportunity with them to make the department look good when I could. As a young cop on the desk, my Sergeant dreaded speaking with the media and instead, instructed me to do so. So, when the local news station, Channel 12 News came to do a fluff piece at the precinct, I was more than happy to oblige. As it turned out, they enjoyed talking with me. The Channel 12 photographer was also there and requested to take a photo of me sitting at my computer on the desk. Sure, anything to help the P.D. look good in the eyes of the public.

They took the shot, and I didn't think much about it, until I began to see the photo showing up on all of the news stations, and in the print media. Channel 12 had syndicated and licensed the photo, and it was now being used as the go-to graphic for Suffolk County cops busy at work. I started receiving frequent calls from friends in New York City telling me they had seen me on the news again. I thought it was funny that many more people had seen me 'acting' like I was busy at the front desk, than had cumulatively seen me acting on stage.

Suffolk adopts new pregnant policy

Suffolk police institute a new policy for pregnant officers. If you can't do the job, leave!

Female Suffolk Police officers are trying to shoot down a new policy that they say discriminates against them should they become pregnant. As News 12's Connie Conway reports the new policy prevents patrol officers from switching to lighter desk duty when they can no longer patrol. Police Officer Stacey Goodman has been on the Suffolk Police force for almost five years. She's assigned to both patrol and desk duty. But if she got pregnant and could no longer perform patrol duty she would not automatically be assigned to lighter duty. Officer Goodman would be forced to take an unpaid leave of absence and use up all her sick time and accrued vacation time.

Police Commissioner John Gallagher instituted a policy change last month that bars patrol officers both male and female from being automatically switched to lighter jobs such as desk duty when they can no longer perform patrol duty. They must now take an unpaid leave of absence using accrued time-off compensation. That means rookies would have little options but to use up to 57 vacation, sick and personal days accrued. They could also compile up to 150 hours comp time but they could loose health benefits and pay at a time when they need it most.

The PBA plans to fight the new policy all the way. In fact, the union President is in Washington meeting with Justice department Officials and they plan to go to court if they have to. Officer Goodman just hopes the Department comes up with a compromise..rather than have a uniform policy for all. Video

Things were going well for me on the desk, for a while. I started dating a lieutenant who was in charge of the precinct detective squad. We kept it quiet and professional.

Overall, and for reasons I was not always privy to, my direct Lieutenant, the attorney, tended to not only piss off a bunch of cops, but some higher ranking officials as well. When I would be out for vacation or on training, one of the new female hires had been filling in for me on the desk. I had seen her on the road and she did not like being a cop—her husband, who was also a cop, had pushed her into it. She was polite and nice enough, but not really into the job and was not very motivated. It was obvious to me she really did not belong. Then I got a call from an inspector who told me that this female cop had lodged a complaint against our Lieutenant for sexual harassment for a comment that he made. Somehow, my name came up in the matter, that I had heard the comment. No fucking way. I wasn't getting involved in other people's bullshit.

"Nope," I told them. "I did not hear it." I said it because I did not hear it. And there was no way I was going to lie to enforce someone else's twisted view of the universe. Well, that was not enough. Phase two of this clusterfuck was the brass coming around and putting pressure on me. "You sure you didn't hear it?" It was clear they expected me to say I had.

Fuck that—like the guy or not, he had a family to support and I was not taking part in their witch hunt. Needless to say, when all was said and done, the Lieutenant got transferred, I got thrown off the desk and reported for shit duty again, and the complaining female took my spot on the desk. Added to that was the new Lieutenant that came in and wanted to throw his weight around to show everyone who was the boss. Well, this did not sit well with the man I was seeing at the time, and apparently the two lieutenants went out back to 'talk it out' with their fists.

What do I call the Police Department? 'High school, with guns.'

No disrespect to all of the great people who selflessly serve and protect—but I found that a lot of people who get involved in police work don't do it for the same reasons that attracted me to the profession. Bitching, backbiting, undermining and backstabbing were the daily course served up by many gossiping little bitches of both (all) sexes with a badge. I sometimes thought that handing out guns in that line might be a big mistake. While some are bitching that you didn't drop what you were doing and run to say hello to them, others are excluding you if you failed to shun someone whom you didn't realize was on the outs. "You'd better say he did it, or you'll never get another promotion." It's so easy to get blackballed or blacklisted when you're in the middle of a bunch of punk-ass little bitches, that it makes protecting and serving almost impossible. There—I said it. Fuck you! And . . . you know who you are.

The Squad One lieutenant heard that I was available, and liked my numbers, so he recruited me to work for him. Hell yes. The 407-car opened up, and I liked the idea of working in Commack, a residential section of Smithtown. I pushed hard and got the assignment. I enjoyed the post, and worked it with pleasure.

At the time I was a patrol officer it was still a good time to be a cop. The community I served was supportive, and appreciated the work we did to keep the peace. Likewise, I was very proud of the job I had and the service I performed for the community. I was sensitive to the power the county had invested in me, which allowed me to take people's civil liberties away from them. I really felt the weight of that responsibility and knew that stripping someone of their constitutional rights, albeit with due process, was a mighty weight on my shoulders.

One afternoon I had been requested by the detectives to watch a house in Commack. I did not ask why, I just went to my assignment. I parked the patrol vehicle on the curb side of the house. It was winter and the snow on the ground added to the ambience of the quaint Commack neighborhood. A few minutes into my watch, I heard a tapping on the vehicle's window. I observed an older woman standing in the snow with a tray of cookies and hot chocolate in a paper cup.

"I saw you sitting here, and it's cold out, so I brought you something," she said.

Wanting to be polite, I smiled and thanked her and took the hot chocolate from the tray. There was a lot of that kind of kindness from the community; even more so after 9/11, at least for a while.

■ ■ ■

September 11, 2001 — 09:12

American Airlines Flight 77 flight attendant Renee May was able to call her mother, Nancy May, on a cell phone. The hijackers didn't appear to know she was placing the call. She told her mother that the flight had been hijacked, and everyone was forced to the back of the plane. She asked her mother to contact American Airlines, who, as it turned out, was already aware of the hijacking.

A few minutes later Barbara Olson called her husband, Solicitor General Ted Olson, and told him about their circumstances. She said the terrorists had used box cutters and knives to take control of the airplane, and that they didn't realize she was calling him. One minute into the call, it was suddenly cut off, and Ted Olson immediately called the Command Center at the Department of Justice, but had no luck reaching the Attorney General. Olson's phone rang again after five minutes and his wife told him that a voice had come over the intercom announcing that the flight was hijacked, and asked Ted, "What do I tell the pilot to do?"

Ted Olson asked her location, and the only thing she could report was that they were flying low over a residential area. It was at that point that he informed her of the attacks on the World Trade Center. Barbara was quiet for a moment, then as the reality of their situation became clear, she told him that she loved him very much, and he told her the same. At that point, the line went dead again.

Hani Hanjour was bringing Flight 77 in low and very fast, making a straight course toward downtown Washington, D.C. When they were just 5 miles west-southwest of the Pentagon, he made a 330-degree spiral turn clockwise and descended to just 2,200 feet. Hanjour advanced the throttles to maximum power and dove at 530 m.p.h. directly toward the Pentagon. Just seconds from the Pentagon building the plane's wings clipped five streetlamps creating a smoke trail behind the incoming missile.

At 9:37 and 46 seconds, Flight 77 smashed into the western side of the Pentagon, killing the 64 people on board, and 125 in the Pentagon building. The fatalities at the Pentagon included 55 military personnel and 70 civilians. Over 100 more were injured, some very badly, and were taken to local hospitals.

When Flight 77 slammed into the Pentagon, there were a total of about 18,000 people working inside the building. The particular section where the aircraft hit had just undergone a major reinforcement upgrade, which kept most of the damage contained in a relatively small portion of the building.

Chapter 9 — We All Saw

I was a Suffolk County police officer with six years on the job, and I had just finished my 4:00 p.m. to midnight shift on Monday. My patrol car schedule consisted of rotating tours of duty from 8:00 a.m. to 4:00 p.m., and 4:00 p.m. to 12 midnight. I had just completed five night tours, and was going to enjoy the next 72 hours off, and would return to work Friday morning at 8:00 a.m. A police officer's schedule makes it nearly impossible to have a social life.

I woke up Tuesday morning and remembered that it was primary day—I needed to go vote. It was an unseasonably warm September morning for the northeast with clear blue skies. I had things to do, so I showered, dressed and jumped into my personal vehicle to run a few errands around my Long Island neighborhood. I always left the radio on in the car, because when the car was on I liked the music on. I waited for the music, but instead heard some on-air talk about the World Trade Center and wondered if it was the anniversary of the 1993 bombing when Islamic terrorists exploded a large car bomb under the towers. I pointed the car toward the post office and waited for my music to come on, thinking for a moment that the 1993 WTC bombing actually took place in February. It was mid-September now—so it could not be the anniversary. The chatter that interrupted my music began to take shape in my mind and I was beginning to realize that something was not right about the situation. By the time I reached the post office, it seemed clear that there might be some kind of situation developing at the World Trade Center in New York City. Initial reports were that it was a small private plane, I heard the words twin engine plane, but there was talk that the gaping hole in the building was fairly large.

I turned the car around and headed back in the direction I'd come from, back towards the precinct. I thought I might get better information there. I pulled into the parking lot and walked into the main entrance of the precinct. The desk officer stood and looked, and recognized me and buzzed me in. I walked down the hall to the Crime Control office. Crime Control were plainclothes police officers who did investigations and handled street crimes and were a great asset to both patrol and the detective squad. The officers that were there were watching the events unfold on a small TV in their office.

"What the hell is going on?" I asked, directing the question to one of the guys I recognized.

He just shook his head; unsure, like the rest of us. Looking at the TV, I thought the gaping hole in the North Tower looked too large to be a private plane. Just as we had our eyes focused on the TV trying to figure things out an airplane appeared on the screen and careened toward the towers and within a second crashed into the South Tower. We watched in disbelief as the reality struck us all—this was no accident. This was a concerted attack.

We watched the screen in stunned silence. I had tunnel vision, and was locked on the screen, seeing and hearing nothing around me. It was like watching a train wreck before my eyes, moving in slow motion. My brain had trouble processing what my eyes were seeing. I was a cop, and as such, I was fairly familiar with the reality of evil that exists in our world. I had seen it in various forms and places in my career.

This was more. This was evil on a scale I hadn't heard of outside of war.

The possibilities swirled through my mind as I tried to understand who was doing such a terrible thing. The reality that people were in the building where the plane hit passed through my mind as I wondered how many additional victims had been on the airplane. All those lives snuffed out in an instant. It was horrific. Gut wrenching. The commentators on the television must have been having the same thoughts I was, and I began to hear people in the room find words to express their confusion and the inevitable conclusion—this was a coordinated attack planned by an enemy.

The next thing that came to mind was . . . is it over? Is there more? What's still to come? With that in mind, the question came to me—what's *my* next step? I was a cop. Serve and protect. It was obvious that protection was suddenly high on the list of needs of those nearby. The melee at the World Trade Center was the immediate problem. Would the damage get worse? Were there additional targets? If so, how many?

One thing I knew was that America's innocence had just ended—in that very moment. I heard occasional expressions of disbelief and then silence in the room, but nothing took shape in my brain. I glanced around the people in the room, and the feeling came over me that I had to go—go do something. I rushed out of the room and down the hall and made a left, and went into the uniformed Lieutenant's Office. The Lieutenant was standing in the corner of his office looking at a small television.

"Is there something I can do?" I asked. "Are you sending people out?"

"I don't know," he shook his head. "I don't know what is going on. I don't know if they'll call people in—or anything." I looked at him, and could tell that he was calculating the extent of the attack and its damage, and whether the crisis would reach Suffolk County, or if we would need to pour into the city to help there.

I looked at him for another moment, then said, "Look, if you need me, I'm available."

He nodded his head then looked back at the screen on the small TV. The commentators were talking about the possibility of other attacks—perhaps across the nation. Everyone was holding their breath to see what would happen next.

I left the precinct and got back into my car, and drove home where I was fixated on the screen for the next few hours.

＊ ＊ ＊

In late 2003, I was working in a marked patrol car in the hamlet of Nesconset, located in the town of Smithtown. I went on the assist of another unit responding to a bank robbery call at a local bank branch. Bank robberies are the jurisdiction of the FBI, although local police are usually the first on the scene, followed by a police detective and a supervisor.

These bank robbers had hit a number of local banks and had used the same M.O. at all their robberies. They were described as two Hispanic males, possibly with facial hair. I was not privy to any bank video footage, but was always paying attention to what was happening. On a couple of occasions I had heard tellers giving bits of information, such as the type of vehicle, or one teller who insisted the vehicle had a broken taillight, but could not recall anything else. Another teller at a different bank robbery scene had reported that the vehicle was an unusually small pickup truck.

Separately, these descriptions were not that helpful. Together, they were. I had made a mental note about both details.

In late October I was patrolling a little east of Smithtown in Lake Grove, heading northbound and stopped at a traffic light. I noticed that in front of me was a weird little white pickup that reminded me of a clown car. As I was thinking about what the bank teller had said, my eyes focused to see if the truck had a broken taillight. Bingo! It was a little Isuzu Pup pickup truck.

I got on my radio and told the dispatcher that I was going to make a traffic stop for a vehicle answering the unique description of the bank robbers, and I needed immediate backup. I gave them the make and model of the truck, along with the plate number. I owned these bastards now. I heard the call for backup go out as the light changed and we all started to go. I turned on my lights and pulled the pickup over to the side of the street. I bided my time, expecting my backup to arrive at any moment, but no one came. I had a tiny waist, which I adorned with a Bat Utility Belt filled with equipment—drawing the nickname Inspector Gadget from the other cops at times—so I grabbed my cutting-edge flip phone and called in and told the boss that I had the bank robbers pulled over, and I needed immediate backup.

"All right," he said. "Sit tight. I'll get a couple of detectives out to you ASAP."

I finally decided I needed to get out of the car and walk up there, or they would get too suspicious and take off. I pretty much expected to find two mustached Hispanic males sitting in the small truck, but as I got up to the driver's window I could see that they were wearing heavy, dark makeup and phony mustaches.

"Hey guys. How's it going?" I greeted in my friendly cop voice. The driver was a little nervous, so I said, "What's with all the makeup?" Their makeup was very good—professional stage makeup.

The passenger was slicker, and said, "Oh, we're going to a Halloween party!" He had no Spanish accent, of course.

"Oh, how nice," I said, smiling broadly. Then I added, "Where's the party?"

"Uh, in Smithtown," the passenger said. I could see the driver was very uncomfortable with our friendly discussion.

"Oh. What street?"

"Oh, uh, uh," the passenger stammered, and mumbled something that I assumed was a street in Smithtown.

"Could I have your license and registration, please?"

The passenger reached over the driver and handed me the PBA card of a cop I knew, whom they said had sold them the pickup. A PBA card is a courtesy card, which some people think is akin to a Get-out-of-jail-free card. I took the card and looked at it, and put it in my pocket. Unlike most traffic abusers, this card wasn't getting these two any clemency, and they weren't getting it back.

When they saw me tuck away their PBA card, the passenger, who was obviously the brains of the operation, piped up and said, "Well, what did we do, anyway? Why did you pull us over?"

"Well," I stalled, "you have a broken taillight, for starters. Now—license and registration." I looked at the passenger over the driver and said, "Do you have I.D. too? I want to see your I.D."

I watched the driver fumble nervously for his wallet and license and I glanced around to see where the hell my backup was.

"A broken taillight?" the passenger replied. "You pulled us over for a broken taillight? We'll get it fixed."

The driver handed me his license and the registration, then pulled out a cigarette and a lighter. Now it was time to start poking and prodding a little, to see what squished out. The driver lit his cigarette while I spoke and pulled it away from his lips as I was talking. He was returning it to his mouth when I said, "You know, your distinctive vehicle is very similar to one seen leaving a number of bank robberies in the area." As I said this, he jerked and put it up his nose.

I smiled as I watched him pull away the cigarette with the dark makeup ring around the butt.

The passenger pulled his license from his wallet and handed it to me, and coolly said, "Well, so many cars look alike."

"Yeah. You're right," I said in a friendly tone, to keep them calm. Although I knew there was no way they could outrun me in that tiny squirrel-mobile, I didn't want them to try it, and endanger the other drivers on the road—or worse; pull a gun and shoot their way out. I took their licenses and registration back to my car.

After a couple of minutes I saw the detectives pulling up behind me in their car. Finally! I got out and gave them a quick briefing, and said, "These are the bank robbers. You can take that to the—uh, well, they're the guys."

They said okay, and went up to the two front windows and questioned the two suspects. They returned to me after a couple of minutes and said, "Write them your ticket, then let them go."

"Let them go?! But these are the bank robbers. They've got their fucking makeup on. They're on their way to a heist right now!"

"Yeah. Calm down," one of the detectives said. "We've got the robbery squad on them already. They'll follow them around and get the evidence we need to put them away. Unless we catch them in the act, it's really hard to put together the proper proof that it was them behind the makeup in the banks. Their licenses are good, and the car is good. We need to make sure and get all our ducks in a row, so they don't get off on a technicality. You did great work. We know who they are now, and we've got them. You just issue the summonses and let us take care of the rest."

I finished writing the summonses as the detectives pulled away. I took them up and handed them to the driver, with their licenses and registration, and said, "Okay, looks like everything is clear. Just a case of mistaken identity. But I'm citing you for the broken taillight, the extra plate in the back of the truck, and the other infractions we discussed."

They happily took their tickets and drove away. Instead of just considering themselves lucky for avoiding arrest on felony bank robbing charges, the duo drove back home, then decided they wouldn't be skunked by a fluke like a random traffic stop. They took their gun and drove to Nassau County to rob a Bank of America there.

When I discovered that, I was furious, because I knew who would get blamed if someone was injured in an armed robbery—the cop that had them, but let them go. The bank teller in Nassau County pushed the robbery alert button during the robbery, and a canine unit was very close to the bank. As the alarms went off the robbers were forced to run as they saw the canine cop approaching. The cop and dog chased them down and captured them.

A couple of days later I arrived at work and was greeted by a few of my bosses, who were glowing. "Well, here's the hero who brought down the notorious bank robbers."

"What?" I had no idea why they were all there. Another Sergeant handed me a press release compiled by the Robbery Squad, just released by the Department of Public Information Unit. The press release cited the very "astute" patrol officer that had identified two bank robbers that led to their ultimate arrest.

They were charged with two counts of robbery in the first degree, and one count of criminal possession of a controlled substance. It turned out that the Robbery Squad had followed the suspects using the information I provided, and also caught them in the act of purchasing heroin with the money obtained from the commission of the bank robberies.

The FBI supervised the case, but let Suffolk County and Nassau County handle each of the several robberies at the local level. The Suffolk County Robbery Squad detectives had written a glowing report about how I had collected the clues about the bank robbers and had spotted them and gotten positive I.D.s on them. In their statements, the bank robbers told the FBI that they were headed for my personal bank—the Commack Bank of America—when I pulled them over. They changed their plans as a direct result of my actions, and that's what got them caught.

My boss got a call from the local newspaper asking about the cop who helped capture the bank robbers. He ordered me to do a phone interview, which I did. The reporter seemed more interested in finding out about my personal life than the actual story itself.

The FBI later came to the precinct to present me with an award. It was quite a nice little ceremony with mostly bosses at the 4th Precinct. I was also made Cop of the Month for

January 2005, as a result of this incident. Spotting that little clown car with a broken taillight was a proud day for me.

TOP COP

Officer Stacey Goodman of 4th Pct.

For recognizing the car identified in a series of bank robberies, Officer Stacey Goodman was named the Fourth Precinct cop of the month.

Goodman was on patrol Oct. 22, 2003, when she saw a car matching the description of one used in bank robberies in Nesconset and Lake Grove. Goodman pulled it over.

"It fit the description," said Goodman. "As soon as I approached the vehicle, I had a pretty good feeling" that it was the right men. For one thing, the two men in the car were wearing full makeup, including mustaches and beards drawn with black makeup.

As she talked to them at the traffic stop, Goodman noticed the two men were nervous answering her questions. She called the precinct's detectives on the bank robbery case, and they advised her to write a traffic ticket and let them go since there wasn't enough information to arrest them at the time.

With the information Goodman obtained, including names and addresses, detectives arrested the men the next day.

Goodman said that on the same afternoon, the two sus-

Officer Stacey Goodman, Fourth Precinct cop of the month

pects robbed another bank in Hicksville. When detectives arrested them, they were buying heroin with the money taken in the robbery.

Goodman, with the department since 1995, has two headquarter awards and one previous cop of the month honor.
— STACEY ALTHERR

U.S. Department of Justice
Federal Bureau of Investigation

Police Officer Stacey Goodman

The FBI extends its appreciation for your outstanding assistance in a joint investigative effort. Your contributions were immeasurable, and you have the gratitude of the FBI for all you did to help accomplish the objectives of the investigation.

You can be proud of the role you played, and I join my associates with whom you worked in congratulating you on a job well done.

November 2003
Date

Robert S. Mueller, III
Director

＊ ＊ ＊

September 11, 2001 — 09:50

United Airlines Flight 93 Passenger Lauren Grandcolas called her husband and left a message, then gave her phone to Honor Wainio. Wainio called her stepmother told her what was happening to them on the flight, and finished, "I have to go. They're breaking into the cockpit. I love you."

Todd Beamer told GTE phone operator Lisa Jefferson the group was planning to "Jump on the hijackers and fly the plane into the ground" before the hijackers could complete their mission. Beamer asked Jefferson to pray with him. He began:

Our Father, who art in heaven, hallowed be thy name; thy kingdom come; thy will be done on earth as it is in heaven. Give us this day our daily bread; and forgive us our trespasses as we forgive those who trespass against us; and lead us not into temptation, but deliver us from evil. Amen.

He continued and recited Psalm 23, and others around him on the plane joined him:

The Lord is my shepherd; I shall not want. He maketh me to lie down in green pastures: he leadeth me beside the still waters. He restoreth my soul: he leadeth me in the paths of righteousness for his name's sake. Yea, though I walk through the valley of the shadow of death, I will fear no evil: for thou art with me; thy rod and thy staff they comfort me. Thou preparest a table before me in the presence of mine enemies: thou anointest my head with oil; my cup runneth over. Surely, goodness and mercy shall follow me all the days of my life: and I will dwell in the house of the Lord forever.

Beamer then made a final request of Jefferson. "If I don't make it, please call my family and let them know how much I love them." Jefferson agreed, then heard voices and Beamer answered, "Are you ready? Okay. Let's roll."

At 10:00 a.m. the passengers grabbed anything they could use as shields or weapons—trays, utensils, plates, glasses and bags—and they all rushed forward together, attacking the terrorists standing guard outside of the cockpit. The terrorists screamed out in pain as the passengers injured them in the violent assault. As they attacked, the terrorist pilot Ziad Jarrah asked loudly, "Is there something? A fight?" The guard inside the cockpit with him held the door closed. Jarrah pulled on the yoke and maneuvered the plane aggressively on its left, throwing everyone around the cabin. "They want to get in here," he exclaimed to the guard just behind him as he pitched the nose of the plane up and down repeatedly to knock the attackers to the ground. "Hold, hold from the inside. Hold from the inside. Hold!"

Jarrah was able to get the plane stabilized for a few seconds, then he asked the guard behind him, "Is that it? Shall we finish it off?"

"No. Not yet," the guard said. "When they all come, we finish it off."

Jarrah pitched the nose up and down again, and one of the passengers cried out, "In the cockpit! If we don't, we'll die!"

A few seconds later another passenger yelled, "Roll it!" The passengers grabbed the food cart and rolled it forward and smashed it into the cockpit door.

Jarrah steadied the plane and said, "Allāhu 'akbar! Allāhu 'akbar!" He then asked the guard, "Is that it? I mean, shall we put it down?"

"Yes, put it in it, and pull it down."

The passengers continued to rush the cockpit, trying to wrest control of the yoke from Jarrah, who immediately pushed the aircraft into a steep dive. A male passenger yelled, "Turn it up!"

A second later, a hijacker yelled, "Pull it down! Pull it down!"

As the passengers grabbed Jarrah and wrestled the yoke away from him, he screamed in Arabic, "*Hey! Hey! Give it to me! Give it to me! Give it to me! Give it to me! Give it to me! Give it to me! Give it to me! Give* it to me!"

Jarrah pulled the yoke hard to the right and pushed the plane into a steep nosedive as it rolled upside down. The passengers attacked relentlessly, and the hijackers fought back, screaming, "Allāhu 'akbar! Allāhu 'akbar!"

The plunging airplane picked up speed and the hijackers screamed and yelled as passengers broke plates and glasses over their bleeding heads.

After a moment a passenger calmly said, "Pull it up."

A few seconds later, at 10:03 a.m., Flight 93 impacted in an empty field in Stonycreek, Pennsylvania, just north of Shanksville. Everyone aboard died instantly.

Chapter 10 — Activated

The phone in my house rang and I jumped, suddenly aware of my surroundings. "Hello?" I said into the receiver.

"This is the regional Coordinator for D.M.O.R.T. You're being activated. Can you deploy?"

"Yes." I didn't even think about it.

I called the precinct and spoke with the sergeant. "Boss, I've been called to deploy, and won't be coming into work. I'm going to get my orders now to see where they need me." He said a couple of things that made it clear he wasn't sure about my status, so I said, "Look, you can put me on vacation, or on leave—but I'm telling you, I'm not coming back to work for the foreseeable future—at least two weeks."

"Okay," was all he said.

I had a good working relationship with the civilian staff who worked at the Police Department at the 4th Precinct, and when the administrator in charge of attendance found out that I was going to be deployed and would be working at Ground Zero, she notified the secretary to the County Executive, Robert Gaffney, who in turn signed an executive order directing that I should continue to receive my regular pay while I served at Ground Zero.

I was set to deploy the following morning, so I spent the day preparing. I grabbed my go-bag, which was filled with small emergency items like a flashlight, batteries, a Leatherman multi-tool, and other things. I packed my vitamins, supplements, cell phone charger and an extra battery. In 2001, cell phones were not the technological marvel they are today; they had removable batteries and did not usually have cameras. I folded some clothes and an extra D.M.O.R.T. uniform into a large duffel bag. I notified my neighbor that I would be away for a couple of weeks, and he didn't even ask where I was going—he knew what I did for living and had a sense of where I would be. I went to my regular gas station, filled up my car with gas and threw a small case of water into the trunk.

It's nearly impossible to get a pistol permit in New York State, but police officers can carry handguns when they're off duty. I looked at my Glock 19 and wondered if I should take it with me. I was a cop, and this was a time of decimated national security, so that tilted in favor of taking it. Plus, I was not sure if I'd be acting in my capacity as a police officer while performing my duties with D.M.O.R.T. On the other hand, I didn't expect any shootouts during my activation and assumed the NYPD or federal agencies would worry about security. I thought about it for a minute, then decided to put my handgun in my bag and take it along, but not to carry it on my person for now. I secured my handgun in a case then put it into my bag.

The following morning I put my bags and gear into my personal car and drove to the home of one of the D.M.O.R.T. team members, where we received further instruction. We did everything in person, because the cell phone towers had all been taken down purposefully to prevent additional attacks by using cell phones to trigger explosions. We met at the team leader's home. He had been issued a government

Easy Pass, which was a prepaid device you attached to the windshield of your vehicle so that you could get through the toll booths crossing the bridges. We loaded our bags in the back, and when we were all accounted for, we took off, and headed upstate to the Stewart Air National Guard Base in Newburgh.

It was a solemn drive on empty roads. A national emergency had been declared by that time and instructions were that all private and non-essential vehicular traffic was to remain off the roads. We headed West towards the city, crossed the Throgs Neck Bridge, and it seemed post-apocalyptic with no other vehicles on the road. On any given day, over 120,000 vehicles cross the bridge. On this day however, only emergency, military, and those with federal authorization were permitted through. It seemed so surreal to us. We just stopped in the middle of the bridge for no reason. We looked around and watched the smoke rise where the towers once stood. It was beyond anything Hollywood could cook up with their models and CGI capabilities. We took in the scene for a few minutes, then we continued across.

I was the only police officer on the team, which included a female forensic dentist, another dentist, and the rest were other medical professionals. As we pulled up to the guarded gate of the air base, serious looking soldiers with AR-15s took positions on either side of the vehicle and the doctor driving rolled down his window. They asked us who we were and where we were headed. We explained that we were with D.M.O.R.T. and were given instructions to report to the base to collect our orders.

The men looked us over, and it looked like they were about to wave us through, when one of the heavily armed young men asked, "Do you have any weapons?"

"Uh, yeah," I piped up. "I'm a police officer and have my service weapon in the trunk of the vehicle." I expected him to wave us through at my overly candid reply—after all, a police weapon in a bag in the trunk of the vehicle, voluntarily revealed by a 5' 3" woman in a federal uniform should not have set off any alarm bells. I was wrong. The young man quickly pulled up his AR-15 and ordered us out of the vehicle.

"Hey, alright," I said, lifting my hands a little and opening the door to comply. I repeated, "Look, I'm a police officer. I'm going to reach into my pocket and get my I.D. Is that okay?" He nodded. I slowly pulled my shield and I.D. leather case from my pocket. "The gun is secured in the trunk," I repeated.

When the guards were satisfied with my I.D., they wanted me to open the trunk, then step away from the vehicle. I opened the trunk, pointed to my bag and stepped away and let him search the trunk. Once the guards were satisfied the gun was secured properly, they let us pass. As we drove slowly through, the others shot glances at me as the driver steered towards the designated building.

"What the hell—I just thought I should let them know that I had a gun in the trunk. They were going to search the trunk anyway," I said. "Hey, they asked, and I didn't think anyone would freak out." They gave me a few snickers and an occasional chuckle as we drove through the base until we arrived at the specified building. I noticed other D.M.O.R.T. region members had also started to arrive. We parked and walked into the building and sat in a large room with folding chairs. We were not there very long, and got our orders and left. My orders: Report to Ground Zero.

I looked at the guards as we pulled off the base through the gates. I was not upset with the guards. They were on high alert. Hell, the whole country was on high alert. We began the long drive back toward Long Island, crossing the George

Washington Bridge, then the Throgs Neck Bridge, only stopping at the tollbooths and getting a giggle at the Easy Pass given to us by the feds that read "no funds available" at the garden gate. Luckily, there was a lone toll booth employee who also had a good chuckle and let us through. It was those little human moments that would offer a brief reprieve from the reality that loomed over us all. Normally, the travel times would have been much longer, but there were so few vehicles on the roadways that we made it back two Long Island in record time.

As instructed, we grabbed our personal vehicles and drove separately to the Marriott Hotel in Queens. The only roadway that separates the Marriott Hotel from la Guardia airport is the Grand Central Parkway. The Grand Central Parkway is a six lane roadway, three lanes headed east to the Nassau County line, and three headed west to the Triborough Bridge, so when I arrived I expected to see a full parking lot and a bustling hotel foyer. Neither was true. The parking lot was all but empty. Most visitors to the area had left and all the planes were grounded, and no one knew for how long, so people got out any way they could—buses, trains or rental cars. I parked my car, grabbed my gear and locked the door . . . out of habit. I carried my gear inside the hotel. I saw some of my team members and naturally walked over and set my bags on the floor near them. We chatted for a while before one of the feds in charge gave us our room assignments and other instructions. They decided that because I was a police officer, I was obviously well suited to work nights, so I was assigned to work 7:00 p.m. to 7:00 a.m., seven days a week.

The night shift? I'd never worked overnights before. I was not sure how I was going to adjust to working nights, but it didn't really matter—I was there to serve. The night shift it was.

* * *

March 11, 2004, was just two days before the Spanish elections. That morning tens of thousands of commuters boarded trains in Madrid to scramble across the sprawling city to get to work. Islamic terrorists placed backpacks with bombs inside several trains around the city. Within moments of one another, 10 bombs exploded on four trains in three local train stations, killing 193 people and injuring nearly 2,000. The city was in full panic as millions were frightened where the next set of bombs would go off. The attacks were launched by an Islamic militant group with ties to al-Qaida.

The Long Island Railroad (LIRR) carries millions of commuters into Manhattan every day, and back to Long Island every evening. The MTA (Metropolitan Transportation Authority) is the responsible agency to ensure the safety of the railroad passengers. Local police were tasked with checking the parking areas around the LIRR stations and keeping a vigilant eye for safety or sabotage, especially after terrorists had demonstrated their interest in trains and public transportation facilities in Europe. We had always ensured that kids did not play on the tracks, or that no one walked on the tracks, and would remove them from the tracks if necessary. After the terrorist incident in Spain, the MTA authorized local police officers to arrest trespassers on sight—all in an effort to ensure the safety of the train systems.

One balmy evening in July 2005, I had just assisted another unit in Kings Park on a domestic call and was returning to my sector. A summer rain had just begun to fall as the sun was setting, and as I crossed over the railroad tracks I happened to catch a glimpse of someone a couple of hundred feet up the tracks walking in my direction. I was not thrilled at the prospect of walking up the railroad tracks in the rain. Duty called however, and walking on the tracks was not only dangerous to the trespasser, it created a security risk.

I pulled my patrol vehicle to the side of the road by the trees, grabbed my portable radio and got out of the car. I walked over to the tracks and began walking in the sand and gravel beside the tracks toward the man. He looked at me, and rather than continue on his walk, or stopping to see what I wanted, he turned and began to walk away. I sized him up quickly, and could easily discern that he was a Middle Eastern male, mid to late thirties. He was small, especially for a man— no taller than me. He sported a 7-Eleven jacket. A man in a 7-Eleven jacket walking on the tracks alone did not get my radar jumping, but his actions of spotting me and walking away from me is what set the alarm bells off in my head.

I watched as he disappeared from the path into some trees. I knew that path through the trees circled back to the tracks, so I took the shortcut and intersected him on the path. He seemed startled when he saw me, and I decided enough was enough. He had obviously tried to flee when he saw me, and although at the time I thought this was not the crime of the century, I figured I'd better handle it with the gravitas it required.

I took him by the wrists and placed handcuffs on him before he could react. I reached into my gun belt for my portable radio. "Headquarters, hold me out at the railroad tracks with a suspicious circumstance." I could feel my supervisor's eyes rolling through the radio. I explained to the young man why I had placed him in handcuffs as I began to pat him down. The only item he possessed was a little black book that he had in his breast pocket. He had no I.D.—I double checked and nothing but the little black book. I looked inside to see if he had his I.D. inside the book, and all I saw were numbers, all beginning with a 202 area code—I recognized them as Washington, D.C. numbers.

As a cop you learn to look at the individual details, and you learn to look at the big picture as well. There was something about this big picture that felt wrong about this guy. His evasive maneuvers, the looks he gave me—it was all a little exaggerated for a guy skipping along the railroad tracks. Add in the Washington, D.C. phone numbers in the little black book in the pocket next to his heart, and no other I.D. on him, and you start to wonder if there's more than meets the eye.

It was raining a little harder now so I sat him in the front seat of the patrol vehicle and buckled him in. I slid in beside the wheel and closed my door. I pulled out my cell phone and called the precinct front desk. I gave him my location, and asked him to call the MTA police and transfer me to our Criminal Intelligence Unit. Criminal Intel is the police version of a multi-jurisdictional task force. I knew my supervisor would blow a gasket when he learned I had called Criminal Intel about this guy, but I felt there was something more going on with him. I got through and told the men at Criminal Intel what I had, and they displayed a healthy dose of interest, and told me to stand by—they were on their way. No problem.

As we sat in my patrol vehicle I again asked him his name, he gave me a name. I had no way of knowing if it was actually his name, but I wrote it down anyway. Date of birth? I asked. Again, he gave me one. I knew he was lying, because he didn't look 83 years old to me. I looked back at him and wrote it down. As I was writing down the information he was providing, I was looking at him to make sure he wasn't trying to do anything. He wasn't. He was just sitting there staring out through the windshield, with a determined, but defeated look. Then he started praying to Allah. I couldn't understand the words, but I understood the prayer. This guy was nervous. Praying to Allah for walking a railroad tracks? No fucking way. I watched him a moment, then I decided to chat with him.

"How does it feel?" I interrupted him. He stopped and looked at me. "How does it feel?" I repeated. He just looked at me. "You not only got caught—but you got caught by a woman." Motherfucker. I didn't know what he was up to, but I could tell it was big, and bad by the look he was giving me.

He glowered at me, and I knew that if there was any possible way he could get away from me, and kill me on the way out, he would do it. He was pissed. He returned to his prayer. I watched for a minute then said, "Your God isn't going to help you here." I leaned in and repeated, "So how does it feel? Not only did you get caught, but you got caught by a woman." I smiled at him and he showed me teeth that said he wanted to tear my throat out.

An unmarked patrol car finally pulled up behind me, and it was the Criminal Intel guys. I got out of my patrol car and spoke with them briefly. They gave me some instructions as one of the Intel detectives removed the man from my front seat and brought him back and placed him in their car. I turned over the black book and my notes. Just then an armada of MTA vehicles arrived. Aside from their police officers, high ranking officials also arrived. They were taking this way more seriously than the Sergeant I suffered with every day on the job was taking it.

I got out and greeted the MTA officers and others, then went back to my patrol vehicle to await further instructions from the Intel guys. While I was waiting, my Sergeant showed up. By now the whole roadway was blocked off with police vehicles flashing lights and a flurry of activity.

"You should have let the little bastard go," was my genius sergeant's parting bit of wisdom. He took whatever paperwork I had for him to sign and left. I completed the paperwork Intel had asked for. One of the Intel detectives collected it and said he would be in touch.

It was after midnight when the phone rang and woke me out of a deep sleep. It was the Deputy Inspector from the precinct. He had been briefed on what had occurred earlier and wanted to thank me for my vigilance. You're welcome.

The next day while at work I received a call from Criminal Intel. "MTA asked me to pass on a message to you—they want to thank you—you have saved hundreds, if not thousands of lives." Then he proceeded to tell me things about the man I stopped on the tracks—things that nightmares are made of. Evil intentions. Terrorist acts against America. The tracks were the target.

When my Sergeant was notified of the scope of the incident and who the man I detained was, he mockingly said to me, "I guess I owe you an apology." He did, but he didn't mean it. I learned shortly thereafter that a recommendation for a commendation for my actions came across his desk for his signature, but he trash canned it. I've always assumed that had it been a male cop who caught the terrorist planning to kill thousands of innocent people, they would have thrown him a fucking ticker-tape parade.

GALLERY

STACEY
GOODMAN

I was cast in an all-female play of "The Odd Couple" as Murray the Cop. It was when I saw myself in this police uniform for the first time that a vision of myself as a police officer took root.

NEWS RELEASE

PUBLIC INFORMATION OFFICE
(516) 852-6308 or 6309
F.A.X. (516) 852-6524

POLICE DEPARTMENT, COUNTY OF SUFFOLK, N.Y.
30 YAPHANK AVENUE, YAPHANK, N.Y. 11980

December 13, 1999

Incident: Suffolk County Fourth Precinct Police Officers Make Donation
to American Red Cross for Turkish Recovery Efforts

Location: Suffolk County Police Fourth Precinct, Old Willets Path, Hauppauge, NY

Date/Time: Tuesday, December 14, 1999 @ 11:00 am

On Tuesday, December 14, 1999, members of the Suffolk County Police Fourth Precinct will meet with representatives of the American Red Cross to present a check in the amount of $500. This money was collected from Fourth Precinct Officers to be used for the Turkish recovery efforts. You may recall, in September, 1999, an earthquake in Turkey killed over 40,000 people and left at least one million people effected by the quake's damage. Many of the homeless are still living in makeshift tents.

Interviews and photo opportunities will be available. For more information, please call Police Officer Stacey Goodman, 4th Precinct Patrol Section, at 854-8417.
******

Authority: Cecilia M. Clausing, Public Relations Director
Office of the Commissioner/852-6516

CASH FOR TIPS - CALL CRIME STOPPERS - 1 - 800-220-TIPS
PDCS-6119a

Suffolk County Police New Release about money I collected for earthquake
relief in Turkey.

Fourth Precinct Officers Show Holiday Spirit

12/14/99

From left to right are Inspector Thomas Laughlin, Officer Stacey Goodman, American Red Cross representative Janet Von Berg, and Detective Sergeant Mark White.

by Erica Bowers

After a Fourth Precinct Police Officer learned through the media that 40,000 Turkish people died from an earthquake in September, she decided to help.

With her superiors' approval, Officer Stacey Goodman began to collect donations from fellow officers to help aid those in Turkey who, as a result of the earthquake, are homeless and living in makeshift tents.

Goodman said, "I felt it was a worthwhile cause."

With many officers and workers donating to the cause, Goodman soon raised $500, and, on December 14, she and her fellow officers presented a check to American Red Cross representative Janet Von Berg.

Newspaper article about money I collected for earthquake relief in Turkey.

COP OF THE MONTH – OCTOBER 1997

FOURTH PRECINCT
POLICE OFFICER STACEY GOODMAN, #5032

The Fourth Precinct has selected Police officer Stacey Goodman as "Cop of the Month" for October 1997. Officer Goodman has received one Departmental Award during her two years of service.

At about 9:30 P.M. on the night of July 2nd, 1997, two teenage males entered a convenience store/service station in the Kings Park area. After stealing some candy, one of the subjects threatened the station attendant with a BB gun he claimed he had in his possession. An altercation ensued and the subject in question first kicked the attendant in the back and then threw a chair through the window.

Police Officer Goodman responded to the location and, after interviewing the complainant, she compiled a description of the subject. She also gathered enough information to confirm that this person has frequented that location on previous occasions. The Officer furthered her investigation and identified the subject in question. The individual was subsequently arrested and charged with Robbery 2nd Degree.

This Officer demonstrated persistence and initiative in tracking down this dangerous individual. For her efforts, Police Officer Stacey Goodman has been selected "Cop of the Month" for October 1997.

Cop of the Month Award 1997 for Capturing Robber.

COP OF THE MONTH – JANUARY 2005

POLICE OFFICER STACEY GOODMAN #5032

The Fourth Precinct has chosen Police Officer Stacey Goodman #5032 as their Cop of the Month. Officer Goodman has been with the Department since 1995 and has received 2 Headquarters and 1 Cop of the Month Awards.

On October 22, 2003, Officer Goodman was on patrol in a marked sector car when at 0840 hours observed a vehicle resembling a suspect vehicle used in two recent bank robberies. Upon stopping the vehicle, Officer Goodman observed 2 subjects in the vehicle wearing black makeup to appear as if they had mustaches and beards. Both subjects appeared irritated and nervous. Officer Goodman completed Field Interview Reports on the subjects and forwarded the information to the Robbery Squad.

Acting on the information received from Officer Goodman, Detectives arrested the two subjects while they were purchasing heroin with the money obtained from the commission of the bank robberies. The subjects were arrested and charged with 2 counts of Robbery in the First Degree and 1 count of Criminal Possession of a Controlled Substance in the Seventh Degree.

The Fourth Precinct is proud to honor Police Officer Stacey Goodman # 5032 as their Cop of the Month for January 2005.

Cop of the Month Award 2005 for capturing two bank robbers.

Me with my brother Danny at my Police Academy Graduation.

Me in my khaki federal D.M.O.R.T. uniform.

I maintained my love of horses and riding my entire life.

Police Week, Suffolk County Police Headquarters, Yaphank, New York.

Chapter 11 — 23 Nights on the Pile

I was sworn in as a temporary federal agent by the feds. The temporary morgue had been set up at the edge of the Pile on the street-facing side of One World Financial Center. The security near the morgue was very high, and strict. No one, not even uniformed police officers or others with badges, was granted access without special clearance authorized by the feds.

For the first few days on or near the Pile there was no electricity other than what was powered by emergency generators. There was no running water other than what firefighters were dousing the pop-up flames with. All of the infrastructure in and around the Pile was either damaged or destroyed, and for safety reasons was turned off around Ground Zero. Bottled water and porta potties were delivered to the site on trucks.

At the end of our 12 hour shifts we would wait for the van that would arrive with the day shift personnel, and then take us back to the Marriott. We would go outside into the bright morning sun, which would burn my eyes. It was strange working nights; you get accustomed to the dark. The day shift would be briefed then we would hop into the van and return to the hotel. Normally, on missions with D.M.O.R.T., we would sleep in tents provided by the feds, but since no one was in the hotels, the feds had arranged for us to stay in the Queens Marriott.

Three World Trade Center was also a Marriott Hotel. Despite the fact that it was a 22 story hotel that had over 800 rooms, its size was dwarfed by the Twin Towers that stood above it at 110 stories. The Marriott lost many employees on 9/11, and the WTC Marriott was destroyed. The Marriott staff in Queens was painfully aware of the loss, and they knew why we were there with them. I had a strong feeling that was why they doted on us, at least to the extent possible. In the short time when my roommate left for Ground Zero, and I arrived to sleep, they would rush in and clean our room.

Each morning we would walk into the hotel, tired, covered from head to toe in the dust of Ground Zero that we had come to term "tower dust." The stuff would get all over the floors wherever we walked, but the staff would politely point us to the breakfast buffet they had set up for us, so they could finish cleaning our rooms before we went upstairs.

Except for the time we slept, our team was almost always together. Having someone constantly at your side who really understood what you were going through brought us together. I find it interesting that some little habits I formed with the other teammates, I still have today. I forged a close bond with a couple of the guys from other regions that were also cops who worked the night shift with me. We would sit down to breakfast and one of the western guys would always put salsa on his eggs. Being from the East Coast, it seemed a strange combination, but he encouraged me to give it a try. I tried it, and it wasn't bad. Now, two decades later I find myself reaching for the salsa whenever I have eggs. It's a reminder to me of the camaraderie we formed during my time at Ground Zero.

Every morning after eating breakfast and going to the debriefing from the events of the night before, I would make my way to the elevator and take it up to my room, noticing how civilized and somewhat normal everything seemed in the confines of this modern hotel—a stark contrast from the moonscape I had left only minutes before. As I exited the elevator I would head for my room, and walk in to find it clean and made up. There were two queen beds in a fairly small space, but I would ignore the bed and stay clear of anything that could absorb the filth that clung to my hair, skin and uniform.

I would carefully remove my uniform and lay it over the back of a wooden chair, trying to keep the dust from becoming airborne and spreading around the room. I would take a shower—where I would spend nearly 90 minutes attempting to scrub the death and ruin from my reddened skin. I tried to leave the shower earlier, but I just couldn't bring myself to turn off the valve and grab my towel. There was something so cleansing and refreshing about the falling hot water—more than the ordinary, simple task of releasing dirt—that I couldn't bear to step out. It seemed to cleanse the grime from my mind and soul as much as from my skin. It eventually washed away the memory of the night before. The long, warm embrace from the cascading water helped me to decompress and finally relax.

We had no incoming data, and no reports to warn us—but my gut told me that we were swimming in a sea of toxins every minute we spent in that morass on the Pile, and I worried that scraping it from my flesh might fall short of purging it from my body and all of its intricate systems. I worried what long term damage was being done, and even more for the others who worked beside me, and out on the Pile, digging and searching through tons and tons of shattered debris. I especially worried for those who were unwilling to wear the bulky, ugly government-issued masks.

After toweling off I got into bed and went straight to sleep. I'd sometimes try to stay up a little and catch the news, but it was a losing battle. Sleep always found me as soon as I could relax. I woke to my alarm around 4:00 p.m. and got ready to go down to the Pile and do it all over again. It was the same day every day, without variation or relief. The days and nights melted into one very long night. The days became weeks, and I had no idea about time—it was just a blur of repeating the same thing over and over. It reminded me of the movie "Groundhog Day," but as a horrible nightmare.

I was always tired. Always exhausted. No matter how much sleep I was able to get. The grueling reality of devastation and death always filled my mind, and it drained everything out of me. The only exception in my endless night was one shift when we were asked to assist the New York City Medical Examiner's Office, and it was different, and almost felt like a reprieve from the constant stream of death that flowed through the Pile.

After the first week, I was given permission to go to my home during my off hours. I wanted to wash my uniform and my clothes in my Melaleuca laundry soap, so I took advantage of the offer. Others were complaining about not being able to get the grime and smell of the Pile out of their clothing and uniforms. I had heard many actually had to destroy their uniforms after their service on the Pile.

The drive from Queens to my house on Long Island was surprisingly quick. Still, there were a few vehicles on the road. The short break at my house was comforting, but surreal. The reality of Ground Zero had been seared into my consciousness every waking moment of every day and night, and returning to a strange hotel room and sleeping during the day was all very otherworldly. I felt like a recently recruited vampire learning how to seal out the sun's searing rays while I slept and dreamed of the dead. I had a new appreciation for the officers that chose to work the midnight shifts, as we called them, instead of being among the land of the living on the day shifts. Being in my house, a fleeting reprieve from the world of desolation and death, seemed like a sort of recess from war, to which I must return after a couple of hours.

I checked the mail and collected the bills that must be paid. Life goes on—for some. I sent the checks out in the return envelopes and wondered how these simple, mundane aspects of life could ever become normal again.

I was a single woman who had no children to support, and having always been frugal, I spent my money on things that gave me the greatest value for my dollar. I had purchased a BMW (which sometimes raised a few eyebrows), and found a letter from the BMW finance department. They said they were aware of my line of work as a police officer in New York, and that if my service was causing economic hardship at the time, they would not penalize me for any late payments. I also found a similar letter from my financial institution regarding my mortgage. It was heartwarming to know that we, as police officers, were appreciated. It was a message that often got lost in the mail.

I retrieved my clothes from the dryer and folded them and packed them into my bag. I was required to wear my federal D.M.O.R.T. uniform while driving, so I threw on a fresh T shirt, and put my uniform shirt over it. My uniform smelled clean, and I had become so accustomed to the smell of death, I had not noticed how bad it really smelled until after I washed it.

I took a last look at the inside of the house and locked the door, then drove out of my neighborhood and hopped on the Northern State Parkway on my way back into Queens. As I drove I noticed the smart sign read MANHATTAN CLOSED, warning citizens to stay off the roads and not travel westbound toward the city. I looked up and saw military jets prowling the skies in pairs and heard the roar as they flew overhead, patrolling for uninvited prey.

Working nights on the Pile had a few advantages. We were not constantly interrupted by movie stars and pop singers trying to boost their sagging careers in the bright rescue lights of Ground Zero. It helped us focus on the work at hand. In fact, the celebrities and their cameramen came during the days for the most part, and I only heard about visits as I crossed paths with the dayshift workers. I wished, however, I had been present when President Bush visited the Pile and announced to the world that America would repay the evil done in that place.

Although I missed most of the celebrities and politicians, we received reports from the day shift how things had gone, and who they felt was there to help, and who was trying to boost a sagging career. Some of the best reports came in about real estate mogul and colorful financier and businessman Donald Trump. I was told Mr. Trump brought several of his employees to Ground Zero and spent hours near the Pile and helped where they could, and serve meals to the workers, at Mr. Trump's expense, and did not stop until all the workers were fed. I started watching him at that point, taking an interest in his activities. When he announced his run for the presidency, I heard many people opine that it was just a stunt of some kind, but I knew better. He was a serious man, and he had a real interest in the welfare of American workers.

It was an honor for me to work with men and women who were taking such risks to search for the missing and dead on the Pile. I didn't feel the need to be thanked by anyone in particular. However, one night, when no network cameras were present to hail the event, we were outside the confines of our high security area and were approached by singer Alanis Morissette. She seemed sincere when she thanked us for our service, and I felt her effort was genuine. I let her sign my yellow helmet.

There were many specialists and professionals who volunteered to come down and help us at Ground Zero. There were times when workers needed a therapist to listen to, or a massage specialist to help work out some well-earned tension. People from a variety of professions volunteered their time and services to aid first responders and other volunteers working on the Pile.

The Spirit of New York was one of the regular day cruise ships in the harbor, and was docked just behind One World Financial. After a few days the ship's operators opened it to rescue and recovery workers, supplying meals and professional services. It was really very generous of them. I was told by some of the other workers that the ship was serving the world's best Mac and Cheese. On a slower than normal night where we could get out of the tent and grab dinner, a couple of the guys from my team and I walked to where the ship was docked. Everyone working at Ground Zero was issued a special I.D. badge, which always had to be visibly displayed, so I knew we could leave the secured area and return as long as we had it on us. We walked over to the dock, and before boarding the ship, we had to step into large heavy plastic trays of water to remove any dust from the bottoms of our boots, and brush our uniforms off to avoid carrying contaminants onto the clean ship.

We shook ourselves off as we walked up the gangplank and found the cafeteria. We grabbed trays and walked to the serving line and waited our turn, and got some of the famous Mac and Cheese and found some seats. The guys chuckled, and it was then that I realized I was still wearing my Darth Vader style mask, covering my entire face. I laughed and quickly removed it, and started dinner.

Aside from the massage specialists and therapists, there were a number of veterinarians who had also volunteered their time and expertise. They helped keep the search and rescue, and later, the cadaver dogs in good health and high spirits during their perilous service on the Pile. The dogs had been fitted with special shoes to prevent there paws from getting cut and scraped from the shards of glass, cement and steel. At one point volunteers started hiding in the rubble, so the rescue dogs would find them because the dogs were showing visible signs of depression when no more survivors were found.

One morning as our shift ended, we stood outside waiting for the van to take us away from Ground Zero. People were arriving to begin their work for the day, and I watched them, wondering what heartache and distress they would encounter as they gave their service to the fallen that day. As we stood waiting, a small green feathered bird flew close and landed on some debris nearby. I smiled a little to see it was a parakeet of some kind, and wondered what it was doing there. The thought passed through my mind that it must have been the pet of someone in a nearby building, but managed to free itself. Its bright green feathers were a stark contrast to the monochrome landscape we lived in. As others around me began to notice the bird, I watched as it suddenly fell and landed in the lap of one of my teammates, who had found a chair to sit in while we waited. I was surprised because I had never seen a bird just fall like that before—especially into the lap of a human. We stared for a brief moment, then someone shouted, "We need a vet over here, quick!"

I turned toward a veterinarian station and saw people stop what they were doing and heads popped up like curious deer. Within seconds one of the vets was scurrying across the dusty street toward us as if a fallen hero needed immediate CPR. When he arrived, he saw the limp bird in my teammate's lap. He went straight to work assessing the bird's condition and administering relief and reviving the little creature. I was amazed at the vet's devotion. He was going to save a life—any life—something that had evaded us all since the first few survivors were rushed away from this scene weeks earlier.

The van pulled up and we reluctantly crawled in and took our usual places, watching through the tinted windows as we pulled away, trying to see if the little bird made it or not. In the midst of all this death, saving a life was of tremendous importance. This little green life mattered, and I think silent prayers rose up to heaven on clouds of dust and ash that morning, all focused on the well-being of that little bird. I know mine did.

* * *

The Disney people realized there would be a lot of stress related to service on the Pile, so in April of 2002 they issued a limited number of what they termed "Hero Passes," and invited first responders and their families to join them at Disney World in Orlando, Florida. The park passes would be free, and they gave us half price hotel packages as well. There was a caveat that came with the generous offer from the company; while on Disney properties we would wear a special button they provided so their staff and cast members could easily recognize us.

I invited my family, and most of them passed because they had work and other commitments. My sister came for a couple of days and spent the night at the hotel with me. It was, as promised, a great stress reliever, and I really enjoyed the time at the theme park. Of course, a steady stream of Disney characters walking up to me and acting like I was their best friend in the world didn't hurt. I was invited to have lunch in the castle, normally a very long wait list, which made it extra memorable. Because I wore the hero button, other visitors at the park walked up and thanked me for whatever it was that I did that was related to relief from the 9/11 terror attacks. It was a great feeling to be appreciated, and years of stress melted away in the warmth of those smiles.

Everyone was an American at that time—the entire nation had been converted to Americanism, and for a while, at least, the artificial barriers that usually kept us separated and at each other's throats were gone.

🛡 🛡 🛡

In late 2006, I was approached by the producers of a new TLC Network television show called "Cover Shot," to be a featured guest on the show. Unknown to me, a friend of mine had already done an episode and was telling the producers about my work at Ground Zero, and that I was a police officer. Cover Shot sought out women with an extraordinary story to tell. The producers were interested and contacted me about the show. The Suffolk County Police Department had to sign off on it, of course, because I was, in part, representing the Police Department. They gave their permission to do the show, but drew the line at letting the show do a ride-along in my patrol car. We went to work and they would spend time primping and polishing you with professional makeup and photography artists of famous celebrities. Of course, I was never a girly girl, so this was all foreign to me, but the professionals with Cover Shot knew just what to do to make me camera ready.

For 22 minutes of airtime we had to spend an entire week preparing and shooting daily. I took a week's vacation and didn't tell any of my coworkers what I was up to. I was not going to let any of the guys know what I was doing, because they would never let me live it down. I assumed they didn't watch TLC, and hoped they would never learn about it.

I was picked up at my home in Smithtown every morning and driven to the studio in New York City, by limousine. I would arrive at the studio in jeans and t-shirt and they would have me try on dozens of dresses and shoes. Think Miss Congeniality—a budding beauty queen looking for a good place to wear her gun—that was me .

I worked with Victoria's Secret supermodel Frederique van der Wal, and the rest of the staff, including a hairstylist and makeup artist who had worked with the likes of Madonna and John Travolta. The photographer would give me the obligatory, "You should give up the cop business, because the camera loves you."

I was happy to have my friends and some family members join me in New York City on the last day of the shoot where they do what they called the big reveal. After taking dozens of pictures of me in different dresses, they decided on which shot they should use for a two story billboard that would be on display in midtown Manhattan for a few weeks. The Billboard read, "New York's Finest." True—I was a cop in New York State—but the implication was that I was with NYPD, and I wasn't. I corrected them on many occasions that I worked for Suffolk County, but they liked New York's Finest better, so for a week I was the New York's Finest billboard girl.

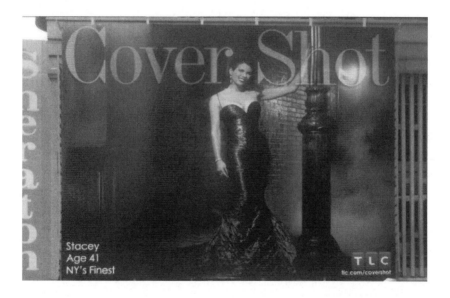

Chapter 12 — Brothers In Arms

I looked through the broken glass of the atrium and into the night. Illuminated dust swirling in the darkness. The cranes were busily at work, like hungry metal dinosaurs picking around in the tall piles of twisted skeletal remains looking for a quick meal. The huge cranes look so small compared to the massive piles of smoldering debris. I stood and watched as they repeated their motion dozens of times— down, pick something up, swing it over and drop it. At intervals I recognized small remaining sections of what were once buildings. The picket fence design of those sections was unmistakable. Columns of narrow cathedral-like arches, rising around ten stories, and somehow managed to convey the feel of a modern structure.

I was pleasantly surprised to see the symbiotic relationship between the New York City Police (NYPD) and the Fire Department of New York (FDNY) firefighters, working side-by-side. Everyone knew about the decades-long antagonism between them and the jurisdictional turf wars and constant struggles for recognition. I was a police officer on Long Island, and I was very much aware that NYPD and F.D.N.Y. were like oil and water. However, in the days and weeks following 9/11 the cooperation and respect shown by the two agencies was inspiring.

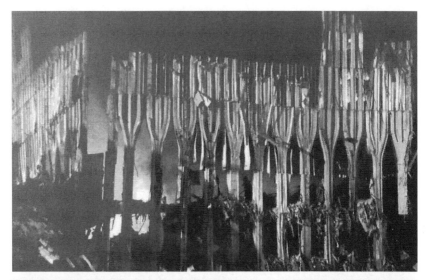

Although I wasn't supposed to have a camera at Ground Zero, I managed to snap a couple of photos of what I was seeing every night on the Pile.

Similarly, I noticed that nearly all Americans became closer and more united in the days and months following the attacks of 9/11. There were very few arguments about who had done what and why they did it. Islamic extremists who hate the Western way of life and the liberties and opportunities it affords its citizens are abhorrent to a political and theocratic system that forces everyone to bow at the altar of their religious extremism. Freedom to worship, and to speak out, and to live life in peace are a direct threat to the totalitarian intolerance of the ancient world autocrats who hide their women behind closed doors and heavy garments, and bind their populations with religious edicts that keep themselves in absolute authority over the whole. All of the sophistry and lies that had protected them up to that very moment now fell away like black blinders into gray dust and ash. We all knew who they were, and what they were. We were united, as a people, and in our resolve to ensure our safety. Political differences melted away in the heat of the burning Towers that day, and we were all Americans, an stood united against our attackers and anyone who gave them any degree of support.

One night I stepped away from the morgue tent to stretch my legs, and the wind picked up quickly and was stirring up a lot of dust. I wore my helmet and mask, and looked something like an astronaut walking on the moon. I suddenly felt stinging in my eyes, and it was awful. I tried to open them, but the very act of moving my lids made it feel like I was grinding tiny shards of glass into my eyeballs.

Two workers who happened to be nearby saw me, and ran over and grabbed me, and escorted me to the medical tent. The doctors saw what was happening and put me on a table on my side, and began rinsing my eyes to wash the ash out. They kept telling me that I had to open my eyes so they could get to the ash and rinse it out, but it stung so badly it was impossible for me to open them at all. They kept trying to flush the particles away and I kept forcing my eyes open as much as I could, and we eventually got them cleaned out. They put some antibiotic drops in my eyes and told me to keep eyedrops in them for the next few days until they were healed.

When I returned to the morgue, I located a pair of goggles that a company had donated for us and were kept in the supply tent. Oh, I was not a pretty sight by any means—I had the bulky space alien mask covering half my face, the goggles covering the other half, all capped off with the giant yellow safety helmet we were required to wear it all times on the Pile. If you saw Marty McFly appear to his father as "Darth Vader, an extraterrestrial from the planet Vulcan," and blasting Van Halen music through headphones—that was my general look on the Pile.

⬤ ⬤ ⬤

I saw movement from the corner of my eye and turned toward the morgue entrance. Four firefighters trailing a swirling cloud of ash carried a basket inside containing the lifeless body of a firefighter. I had seen this before—dozens of times before—but it never became routine.

Firefighters wore prominent name tags on the back flap of their turnout gear, and as I glanced at theirs, it struck me that those of the three men carrying the fallen firefighter were the same. I looked at their faces as I tried to make sense of it, and although they were covered with dirt and ash, I could see the resemblance. That's when it hit me that they were family. *Oh my God*, I thought, my eyes shooting down to the dead firefighter as they gently removed him from the basket and placed him on the steel examination table. There it was. The same last name on his turnout gear as well.

I looked back up and it faces of those bearing their brother, and I felt the heat boiling up from inside me, trying to find escape in my eyes. My lips were suddenly dry and my throat burned. I caught the eye of the shortest of the men, and I could see his reddened eyes watching me intently. I wasn't sure what to do but my routine and the process was to say, "I'm sorry for your loss." I had too much difficulty getting the words out, choking a couple of times before I got to the end.

The youngest brother's eyes filled with tears, but he smiled, and I got the feeling he was doing his best to offer me some quantum of comfort. I felt a keen sense of duty to show as little emotion as possible on the rare occasion when meeting with friends and family of the fallen. It somehow seemed like the right thing to do. Quiet dignity and respect were what the solemn occasion demanded. That's what I thought. It was nearly impossible to maintain my detached composure in this moment, however. My eyes and throat were stinging, and my entire body conspired to make me cry. My spirit said no, and I summoned every ounce of strength I possessed to fight the tears that pounded at my eyes for release. I would not cry. Now, I can't stop crying. I wanted to grab that young firefighter and hold him, comforting him and his brothers in this moment of despair. I didn't. I was professional. I was strong. I was dignified. Perhaps I was wrong.

When you're in the middle of a crisis of massive proportions, your mind tries to help you get through the endless parade of death and devastation by closing out much of the detail, and only focusing on the immediate task at hand. Like so many others, my 23 days on the Pile tended to be a blur in my mind, as death, destruction, death, destruction, death and destruction filled all my senses and pounded at my sensitivities. It was incessant and endless, day in and day out. A steady stream of devastating loss and bereavement. My brain did everything it could to protect me from the psychological injury that such trauma can cause. Then, for two decades we speak only of the big picture—the positive aspects of mutual regard and support, and the combined efforts made toward a common cause.

Now, 20 years later, it has been a harrowing journey to relive the details of every ash covered face and mangled corpse that belied the happy, full, productive life filled with love and friendship right up until the moment the terrorists attacked our city. Trying to recover those details for the sharing of this story has reopened long since 'healed' wounds—scraping off the protective scar tissue that had formed to safeguard the vulnerable injuries that resulted from exposure to such devastation.

My hat is off to all those who learn to deal with death and desolation, and who pursue careers that land them in the middle of the battle on an almost daily basis. These are first responders, soldiers, medical professionals and medical examiners—and many more. All of these find a way to cope with the endless trauma and devastation. Some, better than others. I know that tapping a cop from the cushy suburbs and rushing her into the heart of chaos for any length of time takes its emotional toll, leaving deep scars. The physical damage inflected by exposure to toxins likewise does its own brand of damage. Combine the two, and you have a person who would rather forget than relive the trauma every day. Yet, every night I go to bed and have to place my CPAP machine over my face so I can breathe during sleep—it is a vivid and concrete reminder, and there is no refuge of ignoring and forgetting.

* * *

I got the call on my phone—it was the precinct. They were pulling me off the Pile. After 23 days, I was done. The precinct wanted me back. I would return to patrol duties. Nothing seemed farther from my reality at the time—patrolling neighborhoods in a sector car seemed like a lifetime away.

D.M.O.R.T. conducted an exit interview, which was similar to the briefing meetings we had before going down to the Pile each night. This time I was not paying much attention to what was said. I did not want to leave, and I felt my work was not yet finished. They thanked me for my service and said they were sorry to see me leave, but understood that I was needed back at the precinct. They offered me psychological assistance. Those types of offers of assistance were new in my world, and I just shrugged and returned to my normal life. I did notice, however, that I tended to see things much differently than I had before my experience at Ground Zero. The problems that drove people to commit crimes and hurt others seem too minuscule in my mind. They understood nothing about trouble and pain. They knew nothing about deep human needs. They were just bitchy, whiny little take, take, take bastards who threw a tantrum every time they perceived people or society weren't giving as fast as they could take. I was impatient with their self-centered view of the world. It pissed me off dealing with their selfish bullshit.

I also found that I felt alone. Isolated. The camaraderie I had developed on the Pile with others, struggling to get through the crisis, was beginning to fade—they were becoming ghosts—dissolving with the passing of each new day. I felt the double sense of loss. I started to realize that I was feeling, all be it just a fraction, of what combat soldiers must feel when they returned to the normal world. My God— it's no wonder they find it hard to pretend everything is fine, when in their hearts they know better. With all the troops being processed to go into the Middle East to try to root out the evil that threatened us at the very heart, I worried what things would be like as they completed their tours of duty and attempted to reassimilate into genteel society.

*   *   *

Following my service at Ground Zero one of the lieutenants put in charge of organizing and running a newly formed unit approached me about joining.

"Hey Stacey. How would you like to be our token?"

I chuckled, "That's what I was born to do. What do you need me to do?"

"We need a woman on the new Crisis Action Team. Plus, I thought you'd actually be a good fit. You up for it?"

I enjoyed working with this Lieutenant. He was serious when he needed to be, and fun when it was okay to be. He was knowledgeable about all aspects of policing and was good to the troops.

"Sure boss. What do I have to do?"

"Well, we've got to send you for training. You'll have to travel by plane for this training, and sometimes you'll be traveling by yourself, representing the department, so no crazy drinking at night."

"Check, and check—I don't drink."

He explained where I would be traveling to and that I would be working with other police agencies. I would be training with the newly formed Homeland Security at locations all across the nation. So, I became a member of the Crisis Action Team (C.A.T.), and the newly created

Department of Homeland Security sent me around the country for additional federal training in the event of another major crisis.

When I went for training, I was usually the only female in the large group—sometimes I would meet another female, but no more than that. I managed to enjoy the training and the traveling. The guys running the programs were very respectful and knowledgeable.

The trips would leave my patrol squad a man short, so I put in for the Community Oriented Police Enforcement program (C.O.P.E.) which worked within schools and other social groups to address community concerns and quality of life issues like drugs and street crime, among other issues.

I became very involved in the Crisis Action Team and eventually began to train other police officers for riot situations, formations and tactical control of rioters. All that ended when they promoted me to Detective.

I trained police officers for riot control.

Chapter 13 — Detective Goodman

I was a good street cop. I loved being on the road. I did good work. I'm not implying I was a super cop, but I was a damn good cop.

The bosses wanted me to be a Detective, so I became a Detective by way of the Narcotics Section. My acting skills came in handy for doing undercover work. In 2008, I was officially promoted to Detective. The promotion ceremony took place at the Suffolk Police Academy, in Brentwood, Long Island, New York. It was held in January, and there was a blizzard the night before, and snow was still falling when the ceremony began—so it wasn't well attended.

Much of my undercover work consisted of buying drugs. It was an ugly job, and aside from one or two, many of the detectives that worked in that unit were not very friendly. I guess that's what happens when you do that line of work and deal with that kind of scum day in and day out.

The novelty of buying crack from drug dealers gets old fast. Dressing up in dirty, torn clothing that smells like weed, having unkempt hair, and buying crack from violent felons, some who possessed weapons while selling you junk, turned out to be not so much fun. I was fortunate enough to get out fast and transferred to the General Services Detectives that work out of each of the seven precincts. I went to the 2nd Precinct to start. The 2nd Precinct services the town of

Huntington, from its high end exclusive mansions to what was known as the station—infested with the notorious MS-13 gang, and everything in between. The team I was assigned to had five detectives and a Detective Sergeant, and I made number six. I was partnered with a seasoned female detective. At first she didn't like or trust me—I was dumped on her. I knew people were talking about me and feeding her information, and unfortunately, most of it was misinformation. Again, high school, with guns.

I rolled with it. I tried to learn as much as I could from her at the same time trying to earn her trust. I liked the Detective Lieutenant in charge at that time, and he was tough, but fair. He remembered me from the 4th Precinct as a patrol cop, and liked my work ethic, and we got along great, as I did with everyone on my team.

Detectives rotated tours of duty, or working schedules, just like patrol. During the day tour rotations, one detective would be assigned to on-call duty. If a crime was committed and a detective need to respond to investigate, the on-call detective would be called at any time of the night, prior to their regular tour of duty. I took this responsibility very seriously and I would always prepare the night before if I was on call. I would have my clothes ready and I would go to bed early. I wanted to be sharp and awake in case I was called out.

I found that I was a good detective with great instincts, but I was not a great detective with excellent instincts. I am the first to admit it. I am a well-organized, articulate person, and as much as people think government paper pushers have little practical value, getting all the paperwork right was actually important, and my forte. I had assisted a lot of great cops and detectives to translate their excellent work into perfect paper packages—which was absolutely necessary to stand up to court scrutiny. What I lacked in natural abilities I made up for in acquired skills. Let me clarify—some people are just born with natural abilities to notice the right things and ask the right probing questions that lead to usable information. That wasn't me. To learn those skills, I would pay close attention to the detectives who were naturals, and I would learn from them.

* * *

It was within my first year after working at Ground Zero that I began to notice subtle changes in my body. When I was a patrol officer I had often received letters from my department thanking me for not taking a sick day for the entire year. I was hardly ever sick, so I hardly ever used sick days. I never took personal time off and called them sick days. The bosses liked when you did not take sick days, because they wouldn't have to fill your slot with an overtime officer. My health and lifestyle aided by my arsenal of vitamins and natural cleansers helped. I did not mind the playful jokes from the guys about my "clean living."

As time passed I started to feel my health taking a rapid decline. I was coughing, wheezing and choking for air— especially during the cold winter months. There are some jobs you can do when you're not feeling your best, but law enforcement is not one of them. You never know when you will be called upon and need all of your faculties and abilities to preserve your own life or that of someone else.

Over the years I found myself taking more time off, and my new boss once referred to me as a "sick-time abuser." Sick-time abuser? Fuck you! The fact that I had hundreds of sick days in the bank and was using them slowly was proof enough that he had his head up his ass. I took a breath, let it out, then told him that my general poor health was an obvious result of my service at Ground Zero.

"If that's the case, get a note from the doctor confirming it."

I did. I went to the World Trade Center doctor and got a note, and gave it to the sergeant.

This situation didn't really get better—the assholes seemed to leach from the cracks and things only got worse. At one point in my career I was challenged by a new sergeant in the department who said I wasn't even at Ground Zero, and that there was no excuse for missing work due to illness. "Ground Zero, huh?" he said. "We didn't send you there. There's no record of it," he looked at me like he really had me over a barrel.

"I was called up by the feds through D.M.O.R.T., and the Commissioner signed off on it," I shot back.

"Prove it!" he demanded. I looked at him and shook my head in appropriate disgust. Dumbass. I got the paperwork and proved it.

It struck me as a very odd thing to say, of course. Did he really not know I had worked at Ground Zero? Wasn't it in the record? Did he actually doubt the fact? It's true that I didn't talk a lot about my service on the Pile—as I didn't talk a lot about most of the accomplishments of my life and career. But it struck me for the very first time that organizational memory begins to fade very quickly. "Oh, my God," I thought, "Holocaust deniers may actually believe their own bullshit." How do you prove something like spending over three weeks in the middle of Ground Zero in a high security zone? Photos? They didn't allow cameras (although I had mine on me at times and got some good photos). Plus, I looked like a fucking ghostbuster the entire time I was there and wouldn't be recognizable. That wasn't really proof—not the kind the sergeant was demanding. I had to dig around in my belongings at home and bring in some of my memorabilia and certificates to prove that I had actually served at Ground Zero. After that, I was meticulous about collecting and organizing documentation—letters, certificates, photos and affidavits—because the dumb asses were starting to come out of the fucking woodwork.

The World Trade Center Health Program started conducting audio interviews of people who were at Ground Zero, to establish a lasting record of what happened there.

I was interviewed along with hundreds of others who volunteered to have their experiences taped by the World Trade Center Program. Those interviews, including mine, have been deposited with the Library of Congress to ensure a permanent record was created.

CBS wanted to do something for the 10th anniversary of 9/11, so they went through hundreds of the interviews and chose mine along with five others to cover on the "60 Minutes" news program. I had to get permission from the Police Department to do the interview. Permission was granted and I did the show. The interviews were taped in Stony Brook, Long Island and conducted by Scott Pelley.

Stacey with Scott Pelley of CBS during 60 Minutes interview.

After working on the Second Squad detective team for a couple of years, a slot opened up in the Property Recovery Section. I was interested. The Property Recovery Section supported the General Services Squad detectives to locate stolen items, and recover them. They would do all of the necessary paperwork including statements, evidence, photos, and any supporting documents deemed necessary for the case, and turn it all over to the General Services detectives originally assigned to the case. Steady Monday through Friday tours of duty and all the paperwork I could handle? Sign me up! I was the self-anointed paperwork queen. I was well suited for that job, and it helped that I was well liked by Police Commissioner Richard Dormer. He was a cop's cop. Dormer rose through the ranks to become Police Commissioner. I liked and respected him, and felt he served the county well during his tenure.

I was transferred to the Property Recovery Section, much to the dismay of the Detective Sergeant in charge of Property Recovery. He hated females on the job. I guess when his wife found him insufferable and left him, the fact that she was a police officer probably did not help the situation.

Our 'office' was basically a large closet space with six small desks topped with old-as-dirt computers. I was given a desk and a partner to show me how things were done. With the advancement of digital photography, it made it easier to take evidence photos. We were required to only use department issued cameras. Each detective was assigned to a precinct in which he or she was responsible for property crimes. I was assigned the West End precincts, and became a liaison for the Nassau County Police Department, should they need our assistance on a case. I created a system in which I would create folders for each detective that needed my assistance and present them with all of the documents, printed photos, statements and the stolen property logged into evidence with all corresponding photos and paperwork.

I loved my work there and was able to be out on the road much of the time because I had to travel to the precincts, and did not have to deal with my boss much. I found that most of the detectives were too busy for the little stuff, which I did not mind doing for them. They really seemed to appreciate me, and I them. It was in this unit that I got to meet and work with some amazing detectives, including Detective Stephen Mullen. Steve was a kind and efficient detective. Sadly, Detective Mullen succumbed to a 9/11 related cancer on December 7th, 2018.

On the day before Veteran's Day in 2012 I received an unusual call from a Nassau County Arson Detective. He told me he had requested me by name, and my boss was very reluctant to let him contact me as the Suffolk County detective on the case due to the overtime involved in the case. He had my attention. there was a string of crimes committed on both sides of the county line, and he wanted a Suffolk County detective involved to handle those committed in our county. I drove out and joined him and we began work at 6:00 p.m.

The detective told me about a young woman who was suspected of committing numerous thefts, larcenies and burglaries, including arsons—which was why he was involved. They had just gotten information about the girl's identity, and wanted me to help talk with people in the area with him to track her down. He felt that based on my reputation of getting bad guys to talk, I should be the one to interview her for crimes committed in Suffolk County when we finally got her into custody. It sounded like a great ride to me, so I said, "Let's go."

We looked over the files, and the girl was a typical drug addict—white, lower class, dark hair. We started out in one shithole place, asking questions, which took us to the next shithole, then the next. We were on her trail, and could tell we were closing in on her. We finally located her car, which was full of her shit, and a lot of the stolen items we were looking for, including expensive jewelry. We knew we were getting close to her. It was half-way into the late night when we finally caught up with her and got the cuffs on and brought her to the Nassau County 2nd Precinct, on the North Shore. We put her into an interview room and I was sent in to get the evidence on the crimes she had committed in Suffolk County.

I walked into the interview room and saw her sitting, handcuffed at the table. I assessed her in my own mind first. Her face was surprisingly clean for this type of girl. She'd been driving a car. Those things were a little unusual. She was only half-way to the bottom. It was hard to pinpoint her age. She was unkempt, and looked like she was in her 30s, but her record said late 20s. Hard living.

"You still have the right to remain silent, as the other officers told you," I started. "But if you want to get this behind you, you can give me your statement, and we'll try to get everything rolled into one." She nodded and I sat down. I asked her some questions, and she pretended like she didn't know anything about it. I presented her with photos of what we'd gotten from her car, and a lot of irrefutable proof of her activities, and she just said she didn't know anything about it.

I had dealt with these kinds of people hundreds of times. Some people I would show clear videos of themselves committing a crime, and their response was, "That's not me." She was one of those.

"Look," I said, "let's not make this harder on you than it needs to be." I showed her photo after photo and a pile of records, all proving that she was guilty of several crimes. "You can either lump these in when you cut your deal, or you can play dumb, and have to face a separate pile of charges in Suffolk County. It's your call."

I saw the wheels turning behind her glassy eyes, and she finally said, "Okay. Let's do it." She gave me the information. The Arson detective and I worked together all night, and most of the next day, and cleared four grand larceny and three burglary cases in Suffolk County, as well as many cases in Nassau County. It was a tremendous success. I was disappointed to hear my sergeant bellyaching about the little bit of overtime that went into the case. The money wasn't the problem—the fact that it had been paid to the female detective—that was what hurt so badly. Fuck him.

That case helped me forge a great working relationship and good reputation with some of the Nassau County detectives, so when a high profile missing persons case from Nassau County spilled over in Suffolk County, I was called to assist.

As Property Recovery Squad detectives we monitored the jewelry and pawn shops that bought and sold secondhand items. The Nassau County detectives wanted to recover property that had been sold at a Suffolk County pawn shop. Because Nassau and Suffolk counties have different protocols for that, I was contacted by the detectives and asked to meet them at the store to help recover the items.

I worked with the pawn and jewelry shop owners in my assigned precincts of Suffolk County, and had established great rapport with them, tracking down questionable characters and stolen property through those resources. I took photos of jewelry and other items, and took photos of their records, and collected items that were deemed stolen, issuing receipts to the pawn shops and jewelers. One of the best parts of the work was getting back to the original owners and asking if the jewelry in the photo was theirs. So often the items would have deep sentimental value to them, and they were so happy to learn we had recovered it.

Many people don't realize it, but whether or not a criminal prosecution is pursued in New York is the decision of the victim. If the victim says yes, prosecute, then charges are filed. You would expect them to say yes every time. However, the truth is, that a lot of jewelry and other items pinched and sold from the house are stolen by close family, sometimes close friends. Many of those thefts are to pay for a drug habit. So family is often reluctant to put the offending loved one in prison, and declines to prosecute. If the victim says no, no charges, but wants the jewelry returned, she must purchase the stolen items from the jewelry buyer—the jewelry or pawn shop.

Nassau County had a high-profile missing person, an 85-year-old male. After several days of contacting all of his friends and associates, the Nassau County Missing Persons detectives decided to look up any jewelry that belonged to the man that might have been sold recently. They got a hit. Pieces of jewelry that could have belonged to the missing man were sold in Suffolk County—and they reached out to me. I happened to have a very good working relationship with that particular jeweler, so it was fortuitous that they called me. I called the jeweler and said, "Hey, please hold that jewelry— we'd like to check it out before you melt it down." He agreed.

I joined the other detective and we went to the jewelry store, and found out that another 85-year-old male had brought in the jewelry to sell it. We instantly knew it wasn't the missing man, because they were different races. We checked into the sale and discovered that the man who sold it was a known friend of the missing man. The fact that he lived in Nassau County but sold it in Suffolk County was highly suspicious.

We started taking photos of the jewelry and records, and as I was taking the photos of a ring, I saw something that looked like dried red liquid. "Hey, Detective," I said, pointing to the ring, "look here." She bent over and looked closely, then looked over at me and nodded her head. The jeweler was watching us carefully and as he saw the same thing we did, his face contorted at the thought. Dried blood. I turned the ring on the counter and began taking more photos—but now I was focusing on the dried blood. I got all of the photos we needed and got all of the paperwork prepared, meticulous to ensure a properly documented chain of custody from the seller, to the jeweler, to me, then to the Nassau County Missing Persons Detective.

I later received a call from the Nassau County detectives and learned that an arrest had been made in the murder of the missing man. I would be called to testify. I learned that the missing man was a an elderly white male, who had been killed by his friend, and elderly black male. During the murder trial, the suspect claimed that he had accidentally stabbed his best friend . . . in the face with a knife . . . over 80 times. Worst defense ever.

The fact that the suspect and the victim were of different races wasn't that big of an issue, especially not for me. I saw mixed race crime all the time. As I was waiting at the courthouse for my turn to testify, I saw a large gathering of press and media outside the courtroom and wondered if they were there to cover our murder case. I asked around and learned that the media circus was there to cover the story of a black suspect who had resisted arrest, and was punched by a white cop in the process. The media were there to cover that 'horror story' of white on black crime. Of course, none of them was even slightly interested in the real crime, which happened to be black-on-white murder. I felt that with that type of selective outrage about racial conflict, America was headed down a dark path that would only lead to terrible racial divisions, fomented by those who profit from racial tensions. Sadly, it turns out I was right.

Chapter 14 — A Brief Lapse of Judgment

My partner was on call one night, and when I started my shift in the morning I learned that she had been sent out on a DWI Fatal case during the night. Two brothers were heirs to an aerospace fortune, and one was a drunken playboy with a bad boy reputation. The other brother was a family man who was a reliable, solid citizen. The normally reliable family man veered from his normal course and went out drinking during the night, and instead of calling a cab to get home, decided to drive himself. A young woman was driving home and avoided a DWI Fatal shutdown on the Northern State Parkway on the North Shore by taking a sideroad through the country. She got on her phone and told her boyfriend, "It's so dark here, and I have no idea where I am."

"You shouldn't be on the phone while you're driving. You should pull over, or get off the road," he told her. He heard a scream, then the line went dead. The drunk heir hit the girl's car from behind going very fast. She never had a chance. She died instantly.

My partner was a well-seasoned detective and had done much of the investigative work by the time I arrived at the precinct. The story had already hit the front page of the local newspaper, and there was a large amount of solid and overwhelming evidence against the suspect. My job was to assist my partner in whatever she required, and what she needed was someone to sit with the suspect. He was sitting in the interview room still, handcuffed. The door to the room was open and I looked in. He looked defeated.

As my partner completed her paperwork so that he could make his court deadline, I grabbed a cup of coffee and brought it into the suspect. He was beginning to sober up and I believed he had no idea of the devastation he had caused. I had a strong sense that he was a decent man, and this nightmare was an aberration in an otherwise normal, productive life. To my knowledge he had no priors, not even a parking ticket. I talked to him, and he told me he had a wife and small children at home. It was obvious to me that he was quite distraught.

My direct boss, a Detective Sergeant, stood outside the room with his arms folded and was obviously and rightfully very angry at the man for what he had done. My boss was a tall, stocky man whose looks could be quite intimidating. I could see that he wanted to make the man pay for his crime, and I walked out of the interview room and I looked at him and said, "If you tell him what he's done, you'll need to put him on suicide watch." I had good instincts and I was pretty sure I was right about the suspect, but my boss dismissed me with a grunt.

I dropped off some paperwork at the front desk and in the few short minutes I was gone, my boss had confronted the man, showed in the morning paper and berated him for what he had done.

Damn it!

I knew that most of the lowlifes and violent offenders did not deserve any consideration for the most part, but this man was obviously different, and had a conscience and would not take the news of his crime in the way most of our guests did. I was right of course, and he tried to hang himself.

Fucking Sergeant.

I told my partner I would sit with the suspect, so she could finish her paperwork. I went back into the interview room and sat with him behind the small desk. I could see tear tracks etched into his face. This was the most remorseful man I had ever encountered.

"Listen," I said trying to calm him down, "you have a young family, right?" His eyes drifted up looking at me.

"Yes," he said in a graveled voice.

I paused a moment, then said, "Alright—this can go one of two ways." I knew we already had enough evidence to put him away for a couple of decades, the maximum the law would allow at that time. "We have a considerable amount of evidence against you, and as you have seen, it has made the front page of the newspaper." He lowered his swollen eyes. "You can go out and get yourself a high priced defense attorney and fight this in court. If you do, chances are your family will be put on display. You know how the media works." His eyes stayed glued to the table. "That's one way," I continued, "or you and your attorney can sit down with the Assistant District Attorney assigned to the case and make a plea deal." He still didn't look up at me, but his eyes glanced sideways, so I knew he was thinking about what I had just said. "Look, I can't tell you what to do, and I can't tell you any specific deal the DA's office is willing to make, but these are your only two options that I can see right now."

His eyebrows lowered in his lips tightened. He finally said, "How can I make this right?"

I looked at him a brief moment, then said, "You will have to pay the price by doing time. I don't know how much, but I will tell you this—use your time to teach people to turn their lives around and become better people, who respect others and make something of themselves. Use your knowledge to teach, and do community service if offered. Be a model prisoner. That is all you can do." He looked sideways for a moment and I said, "Your family will be allowed to visit you, and most likely won't be hounded by the press. I would consider making a deal if they offer you one."

I heard later that he had pleaded out. He accepted his responsibility in the young woman's death, and paid a hefty price for his irresponsible actions.

* * *

I was still a fairly new detective in the 2nd Squad when I was assigned a grand larceny case at a local jewelry store in a high end mall in Huntington. A vehicle used in the crime was recovered and transported to our evidence impound. I collected evidence at the scene, and took statements. I requested the store's video and advised our electronics unit to collect the footage. While back at the precinct I was putting all of the evidence together and doing the glamorous part of policing—the paperwork. I was interrupted by my phone, and it was an FBI agent working in the New York City office. They had heard about the case I was working, and told me it matched a string of cases they had been working in New York, New Jersey and Connecticut. When felonies cross state lines, they can fall under the FBI's jurisdiction if it can be proved that the same perpetrators are committing the crimes.

The agent on the phone was very matter of fact and direct. I got the feeling he was bracing for me to put up a fight about whose case it was. He said the case fell under his purview, and listened for my response.

"Okay," I said. "But I'd like to help, because the crime was committed within my jurisdiction." I had no intention of getting into a turf war with the FBI, but I did want to be involved in the case. These guys were pros, and had all the right equipment and data access—and maybe I could learn a thing or two along the way.

The agent was silent for a moment, and I could tell he hadn't expected my cooperation. When he started speaking again, it was in a friendlier voice. "Of course," he said, and we scheduled a meeting at my 2nd Precinct. Prior to the meeting, I made sure I had all my documents in order, and made copies of everything as he had requested. I called the lab to see if there would be any way they could put my evidence at the top of the wait list. Luckily for me it was a slow week at the lab, and it probably helped grease the skids when I said the FBI had an interest in the case.

This case was very sensitive, and would come under extreme scrutiny, so it required that we follow procedure to the letter. We met at the precinct, and I had already had my evidence in order. They got the lab results to me in time for the meeting. The FBI kept me involved in every aspect of the case, including attending meetings at the FBI local office, going into New York City to recover some of the located stolen property in the case. The agent was very amicable and allowed me to assist—and where I hit a dead end with our police resources, they were able to move forward with theirs. We had all our ducks in a row and were able to make the arrests. I learned a lot. The agent showed appropriate respect, and fulfilled the promises of full cooperation. It was an eye opening and educational experience for a young detective, and I was able to utilize a lot of the information I gained in future cases I worked. Cooperation—who knew?

✦ ✦ ✦

D.M.O.R.T. was under the blanket of Health and Human Services (H.H.S.), and that's who I served under during my tenure at Ground Zero. After 9/11 the federal government formed Homeland Security, and D.M.O.R.T., F.E.M.A. (Federal Emergency Management Agency) and other federal agencies and programs were transferred under the new heading of Homeland Security. Tom Ridge became the assistant to the President for Homeland Security. Tommy Thompson headed up Health and Human services. After my wrok at Ground Zero, I received a letter from Tommy Thompson thanking me for my service, followed by a certificate from the newly formed Homeland Security, indicating that I was a founding member of Homeland Security.

Homeland Security

Be it known that

STACEY GOODMAN

is a Founding Member of the Department of Homeland Security, dedicated to preventing terrorist attacks within the United States, reducing America's vulnerability to terrorism, and minimizing the damage from potential attacks and natural disasters.

Tom Ridge, Secretary

Washington, D.C., March 1, 2003

THE SECRETARY OF HEALTH AND HUMAN SERVICES
WASHINGTON, D.C. 20201

MAR 0 8 2002

Ms. Stacey Goodman
50 Grandview Lane
Smithtown, NY 11787-0626

Dear Ms. Goodman:

Thank you for the invaluable service you rendered to the victims of the September 11 tragedies. Your deployment through the National Disaster Medical System enabled rapid action and proficient health care delivery to fellow citizens and non-Americans alike in the aftermath of the horrific terrorist attacks on our nation and the world. I am grateful for your hard work as well as the personal sacrifice you endured to serve those in need.

These acts of malevolent terrorism were not only a profound assault against mankind, but also an attack on the basic human right of freedom of all citizens of the world. I am indeed grateful for the help we have received from many friends and allies. Yet, it is the superb frontline assistance and active support provided by Americans like yourself that I will remember most during this time of healing and recovery in our nation.

The Department of Health and Human Services is committed to the long-term process of healing and rebuilding. Your service has been instrumental in this ongoing process. Our nation is indebted to you for your unselfish contributions.

Thank you again.

Sincerely,

Tommy G. Thompson

I enjoyed my work in the Property Recovery Section. I liked working with different detectives and the steady hours and steady days off. It meant I could actually plan events with friends and not have to cancel at the last minute because of a work related emergency that caused me to stay at work later than expected. When Commissioner Dormer retired, my boss got busy trying to get rid of me, despite all of the positive feedback he was getting from the detectives I worked with. I walked into work on Thursday and with that smug look on his face, my boss said I was being transferred. I was going to the 7th Squad. I was out, just like that. No notice.

The 7th Precinct covered a wide range of communities from serene middle-class neighborhoods to gun and drug infested, treacherous, crime-ridden burghs. I wasn't sure what I should expect, but soon discovered that the cops and the detectives that worked in this precinct to be hidden gems in the county. They were the best of the best—hard working, and driven to do a thankless job many did not have the stomach or guts to do. I loved working here. The detectives were very kind to me. When I first arrived, I was a bit intimidated knowing that these detectives were often selected go on to homicide or other elite units within the county. Not only were the detectives a great group of guys, but they had a great Detective Sergeant. All were very bright, yet humble. Hell—that was a rarity in any profession. They were the epitome of what every detective should strive to be— caring, articulate and helpful. They were willing to teach me what I did not know and treated me with the respect. I was truly honored to work with such highly skilled professionals.

★ ★ ★

July 4, 2016, was my last working tour of my 21 year career with the Suffolk County Police Department. It was the 4th of July holiday, and I was cleaning out my desk, getting my box of personal belongings poised for the ride home. I had closed out all my cases and handed them off to the boss for his closing signature. I looked at the squad bulletin board and it was bitter-sweet seeing that my name was already removed. It was a warm and wet evening, so things were slow, and I would be getting off and heading home, for the very last time, at 1:00 a.m. The rain picked up and was surprisingly heavy.

The Senior Detective was retiring at the same time I was, and the new Junior Detective said to us, "No—really. You can't both leave me all by myself like this." We laughed. I had a nice 'gift' of all of my paperwork that I'd created that would remind him which forms he would need for which cases. I was handing those to him with my instructions when the phone rang. I looked up at the clock and saw it was 10:00 p.m. exactly. It was such a quiet night, and everyone was enjoying the holiday, and I would be off and headed home shortly—I clenched my teeth just a little, hoping the call wasn't something heavy.

The Senior Detective looked at me as he picked up the phone. He scribbled notes and his face became grave, and he shot me a glance. I tensed as I braced for impact. The Detective said, "Okay, we'll be right there," and hung up the phone. He looked at us and said, "Vehicle, head-on crash. Multiple fatalities. Burn victims."

My heart sank, and the young detective got a worried look on his face. I grabbed my summer trench coat and we headed for the door. We jumped into our cars and drove swiftly to the crash site. Patrol officers were struggling to get inside the back of a burning car, and I asked what was happening and was told, "There's a baby inside. They're trying to get to it and get it out."

"Oh my God," I said as I watch the heroes emerge victorious with the crying baby. Thank God. Those patrol officers had literally risked their own lives to save the baby.

I looked around and saw that a young man—or what was left of him—had driven into a car with a family inside. It was tragic. A damn shame.

We three detectives talked to the witnesses and responding officers, and after taking their statements, I was tasked with responding to the local hospital where some family members of one of the victims had gone. Normally, this is a process of sitting down and delicately explaining to the family what happened, followed by lots of tears. I was not looking forward to this. What I had just seen was a true tragedy, in every sense. Facing surviving family members was not how I had envisioned the few remaining hours of my last night on the job.

Many hospitals have a special room where the family can fit comfortably and not be disturbed by the regular bustle of the hospital setting. The rooms are usually small and simple with chairs and a table, and sometimes have a water cooler in the corner—and tissues. But, like many aspects of policing, things do not always go as planned. When I arrived, I was greeted by New York State troopers, who had been called by the hospital staff. Members of the young man's family had shown up at the hospital, and were very angry, and taking that anger out on the staff. The mother of the young man whom I had seen charred behind his steering wheel only minutes before was loudly blaming everyone for her son's death. I knew that was not the case—I could see how he had died, and it was no one's fault but his own. The death of the other family was clearly his fault as well.

The staff had tried to calm the mother down, and the clergyman at the hospital had given it his best shot, and even he threw up his hands. I took a deep breath and walked into the small room. I had seen the eyewitness statements and the computer data, all of which confirmed that this woman's son and his car should not have even been on the road. He was clearly at fault. Yet, she felt the world had conspired to rob her of her precious boy.

Nevertheless, I wasn't going to tell her that her son was to blame for this tragedy—and at that point in the investigation we couldn't even say with 100 percent certainty that the charred body in her son's car was his. I walked into the room and closed the door behind me. My raincoat was dripping water onto the back of my pants and onto the floor. By this time I had been working for more than 16 hours, and had been awake for over 24 hours. I was done—but I had one last task to perform as a Suffolk County Police Department Detective.

The New York State trooper stood silently in the corner of the room, watching to see how I'd handle this. The mother took one look at me and as I began to introduce myself to her, she started yelling at me, "Where is my son?! What did you people do to him?!"

"Ma'am, please have a seat," I said trying to calm her down, even though I knew it wouldn't work.

"No!" she screamed. "Is it my son?"

"At this point," I began, but she immediately interrupted me, screaming, cursing and becoming incoherent. I let her go on for a minute, thinking to myself how I was not going to miss this part of the job. I finally got her to calm down enough so that I could explain what was going to take place. I handed her my business card and wrote the young detective's name and contact number on the back—this was his job now, because tomorrow he would be the lead detective on the case.

I finished with the hysterical, accusatory mother, and then had the grim task of going to the hospital morgue to identify the victims. I walked into the midst of the carnage, and the Medical Examiner brought out a body and said the man had died on impact. His body was severely burned. The smell of his burnt flesh hit my nostrils like a sledge hammer, and I was immediately transported back to the temporary morgue at Ground Zero. It was nauseating and disturbing. I struggled to focus as my mind continued to flash back to all of the victims I had processed on the Pile. The stench was a powerful reminder of everything—the death, destruction, devastation and grief, and it was served up to my consciousness with such a visceral impact.

This was pretty much the same for me. An entire family had been killed—burning in a car, due to a careless young man who should not have been on the road that night. It was too much. I finished up, then went back and wrote up my final report, then went home. I was done.

With 21 years on the job, and 9/11 health issues plaguing me, it was time to retire. I had intended to work for another few years, but I knew if I did not make a change, my symptoms would only worsen. It was time to hang up my spurs and ride off into the West—literally.

I did not want a big retirement party. This was not a celebration for me. I loved being a cop and I loved the camaraderie. For me, it was enough to just be with the guys in my squad, and grab some hamburgers at a small restaurant near the precinct. I felt the sincere respect and friendship of my squad and the men and women of the 7th Precinct. I was honored and humbled to have worked with some of the most talented detectives anywhere. When my squad presented me with the plaque, I cried at their generosity and kindness.

Overall, I knew I had been blessed to work beside and serve with some of the best police officers and detectives anywhere, in one of the best police departments in the country; the Suffolk County Police Department, Long Island, New York.

Chapter 15 — Aftermath

NYPD Police Officer Moira Smith saw the first airliner strike the first Tower of the World Trade Center and was the first officer to report the terrorist attacks of September 11, 2001. She was a 13-year veteran of the force and ran straight into the Towers to help evacuate the workers inside. Officer Smith was last seen heading back into the South Tower to help more people. A brief radio transmission from a female officer calling for help was heard just after the collapse of the Tower, and the recording revealed it was Officer Moira Smith.

When I got back to 'normal' work life after working on the Pile, I attended too many funerals. It was horrible. One I requested to go to, and my boss was gracious enough to let me represent the department with a few others, was the funeral for Moria Smith. She left behind a 2-year-old daughter. I got the honor of standing in the front row of the funeral procession and Moira's daughter stuck her head out of the limo window to wave to us. I was in full dress blues standing at attention, trying not to cry . . . again.

NYPD Police Officer Moira Smith assisting man on 9/11.

There were many heroes of 9/11—those who risked their own survival by assisting others to get out of the burning buildings; those who selflessly rushed into the crumbling Twin Towers to rescue the wounded and trapped; and those on the Pile at Ground Zero who did everything they could to rescue the few survivors, or locate and identify the dead, or to clean the mountains of debris to make way for rebirth. I personally witnessed the many hundreds who worked tirelessly to rescue the dying, then to locate the dead, and then begin the process of rebuilding. So many of them are now dead, or dying, just 20 years later. Even I, who was so meticulous in donning the mask and wearing it faithfully—I have been certified with a multitude of severe ailments including chronic bronchitis, asthma, along with other lung and gastrointestinal issues; all related to damage done during those 23 days working among the dead on the Pile.

Everyone who worked at Ground Zero is in the same boat; the rescuers, the ironworkers, the electricians, the plumbers, and the utility workers—we are losing them at an alarming rate, to cancer, pulmonary diseases, all stemming from being poisoned on the Pile. Even wearing a mask, I've still developed a number of Ground Zero related health issues. I had an advantage that most of my fellow workers didn't have. Vitamins. Don't roll your fucking eyes. The vitamins made a big difference. I took them all, plus minerals and supplements. I started taking them in 1999, and cut back on the use of harsh chemicals to clean and sanitize my life. My doctors at the Mayo Clinic have confirmed that my regimen of vitamins I took before and after my service at Ground Zero is instrumental in helping my body resist the toxins that besieged us in that environment.

I didn't escape Ground Zero unscathed, however. To my knowledge, no one did, no matter how many masks or vitamins were employed. My medicine cabinet is now filled with prescription bottles all lined up like tiny little soldiers that stand at attention and watch solemnly as I take them down one by one. I don't take a single pill that isn't absolutely necessary to keep me as healthy as possible.

The winter months and humidity had the worst effect on my body. My lungs would quiver in the cold, causing me to gasp for air. Asthma was one of the ailments that had afflicted me, and many others who worked at Ground Zero. I had to start using a Continuous Positive Airway Pressure machine (CPAP), every night to assist with breathing while I slept. I still use it faithfully every night. I have to.

I had vacationed in Arizona for many years. I was introduced to the Grand Canyon State while dating Ray. I remember getting off the plane in Arizona for the first time, and feeling the dry, oven-like heat of the desert. I knew this was the place for me. I have since found that the dry, hot climate suits me well and helps with my breathing. No winters to devastate me.

I thought about things for a long time, and my dream was to own an Adobe Pueblo Revival-Santa Fe style home in the desert. I knew where I wanted to take up residence, and set my sights on achieving that goal. I sold my home is Smithtown on Long Island and purchased a house in Chandler, Arizona. Chandler is a large suburb of Phoenix, in the southeast valley.

I got a little antsy after settling into my new home in Arizona, and looked into getting a part time job. I was recruited by Homeland Security. At the time, they were actively seeking retired law enforcement officers who wanted to go back to work. The only part-time jobs available were with the Transportation Security Administration (TSA), so I was hired and sent to the federal law enforcement training facility in Georgia. It was a nice fit and easy going for me. They wanted to move me into investigations, but at this point in my life, I did not want to take on the extra responsibility. I wanted to be able to enjoy myself at work without the added stress. I got to go to my first choice airport, which was Sky Harbor International Airport in Phoenix, which was only a short 20 minute drive from my house in Chandler. I worked with other retired police officers and active duty Phoenix police officers assigned to the airport.

The problem was that I was working in enclosed areas, and I was having too many breathing issues and missing too much work with every flare up. My employer was understanding with me, because they realized I had worked at Ground Zero and suffered from related health issues, but after a little over a year it became too much, and I had to go back to retired life.

I started speaking engagements and teaching kids at schools about 9/11 and the work at Ground Zero. I was asked to speak at the Tempe Town Lake Healing Fields, where each year they plant one American flag for every victim of 9/11. It is usually attended by hundreds of people. The Arizona Republic, the Phoenix and Maricopa County newspaper, was there, and published a wonderful article about me. I was grateful for the respectful tribute.

2A | THURSDAY, SEPTEMBER 13, 2018 | THE ARIZONA REPUBLIC

She could be a 9/11 casualty, but regrets nothing

Karina Bland
Columnist
Arizona Republic
USA TODAY NETWORK

Stacey Goodman emerged from the Brooklyn-Battery Tunnel, where the Twin Towers had stood the day before, and saw debris piled 10 stories high.

Through the smoke, she could make out twisted metal and rubble. The ash covered everything and everyone.

"It was like something from a horror movie set," Goodman told hundreds of people gathered at Tempe Beach Park for a 9/11 memorial Tuesday night.

Goodman, a detective with the Suffolk County Police Department, volunteered with the federal Disaster Mortuary Operational Response Team. With spotlights fueled by generators, Goodman could see people shifting rubble.

"People worked in silence as if they were in a church or synagogue," she said.

Goodman worked 7 p.m. to 7 a.m. for 23 days straight. In the first few days, there was no electricity or water. The team slept on unused body bags.

"What I remember the most and it will never leave me is the smell of burning flesh," she said Tuesday. "It was constant."

Goodman worked in a makeshift morgue, where she helped identify remains.

"I am no hero, and I don't claim to be one, but I worked with many," she said.

Now they are dying. An estimated 2,100 people have died of 9/11-related illnesses such as cancer and respiratory ailments. Experts believe those deaths soon will surpass the number of people killed in the attacks.

"Please keep these people in your prayers," Goodman said.

After she spoke Tuesday, Philip Manning approached her. His brother Terry was killed in the World Trade Center. "I'm so sorry for your loss," Goodman said.

Manning nodded. "Thank you for everything you did."

Goodman retired from the force after 21 years. She moved to Arizona two years ago and works for the TSA at Sky Harbor International Airport.

She struggles with worsening health, but says, "I would do it all over again."

The housing market was booming and I was able to sell the Chandler house, and I moved into my dream home, an Adobe style house that sits on the edge of the Sonoran Desert. My large desert property is like a natural desert zoo of javelinas (wild southwestern bores, or peccary), roadrunners, jackrabbits and bunnies, quail, hawks, owls, lizards, bobcats and coyotes.

Of course, I was afraid that snakes would be the problem, so I set up a snake perimeter in classic cop style. However, I actually saw many more snakes on Long Island. In fact, I've only seen one snake in Arizona, even though I live at the edge of civilization against the Sonoran Desert.

Chapter 16 — I Will Always Remember You

In all, 2,977 people died in the terror attacks of September 11, 2001. That number, of course, excludes the 19 Islamic terrorists who committed the atrocities against defenseless citizens. The victims include the 2,753 killed in the attacks on the World Trade Center Twin Towers, the 184 killed at the Pentagon, and the 40 killed in the crash of United Airlines Flight 93 in Pennsylvania. This number does not include the hundreds of victims whose death warrants were signed when they responded to the call to assist at Ground Zero, and have since fallen as a result.

The terrorist attacks on September 11th, 2001, caused more law enforcement line-of-duty deaths than any other single incident in American history. Our friends at The Officer Down Memorial Page, Inc., have complied a full list of officers who died as a direct result of the 9/11 terrorist attacks. We thank them and share their tribute here. One officer was killed when United Flight 93 crashed into a field in Shanksville, Pennsylvania as he and other passengers attempted to regain control of the plane from the hijackers. 71 officers were killed when the two World Trade Center buildings collapsed in New York City. Dozens more have passed away in the years following 2001 as the direct result of illnesses contracted while working in the hazardous conditions immediately following the attacks in New York. Let us pay tribute to the law enforcement officers, representing 10 different agencies, who died as a direct result of the 9/11 terrorist attacks.

God bless each of you, and those who have suffered your loss for these many years since. I remember each of you.

———

American Society for the Prevention of Cruelty to Animals Humane Law Enforcement, New York

- Special Investigator Diane DiGiacomo

Arlington County Police Department, Virginia

- Corporal Harvey Snook, III

Cayuga County Sheriff's Office, New York

- Undersheriff Stephen B. McLoud

City University of New York Department of Public Safety, New York

- Deputy Chief John P. McKee

Connecticut State Police, Connecticut

- Trooper First Class Eugene Kenneth Baron, Jr.
- Trooper First Class Walter Greene, Jr.

Harrison Police Department, New York

- Police Officer Walter L. Mallinson

Montclair State University Police Department, New Jersey

- Sergeant Christopher A. Vidro

Nassau County Police Department, New York

- Police Officer Brian R. Abbondandelo
- Police Officer Charles Dennis Cole, Jr.
- Police Officer Peter Francis Curran
- Police Officer Peter Martino
- Police Officer Paul J. McCabe
- Police Officer James V. Quinn
- Lieutenant Michael P. Shea

New Jersey State Police, New Jersey

- Lieutenant William George Fearon
- Staff Sergeant Bryan U. McCoy
- Trooper Robert Emmet Nagle

New Rochelle Police Department, New York

- Detective Mark S. Gado
- Police Officer Kathleen O'Connor-Funigiello

New York City Fire Department – Bureau of Fire Investigation, New York

- Fire Marshal Ronald P. Bucca

New York City Police Department, New York

- Detective Sandra Y. Adrian
- Detective I Gerard A. Ahearn
- Detective James John Albanese
- Chief of Detectives William H. Allee

- Detective Sixto Almonte
- Detective Luis Gustavo Alvarez
- Sergeant Alex W. Baez
- Police Officer Curtis Joseph Bako
- Police Officer Karen E. Barnes
- Detective Thomas J. Barnitt
- Police Officer Ronald G. Becker, Jr.
- Detective Aslyn A. Beckles
- Police Officer James A. Betso
- Sergeant Gerard Thomas Beyrodt
- Police Officer Derrick Bishop
- Police Officer Scott R. Blackshaw
- Police Officer Frank M. Bolusi
- Deputy Chief Steven Joseph Bonano
- Sergeant Patrick J. Boyle
- Sergeant William Brautigam
- Police Officer Thomas Gerard Brophy
- Lieutenant Rebecca A. Buck
- Police Officer James M. Burke
- Captain Carmine C. Cantalino
- Police Officer Audrey P. Capra
- Police Officer Madeline Carlo
- Detective Megan K. Carr-Wilks
- Detective Joseph A. Cavitolo
- Police Officer Yolanda Cawley
- Sergeant Christopher M. Christodoulou
- Police Officer Peter D. Ciaccio
- Lieutenant Steven L. Cioffi
- Sergeant Charles J. Clark
- Police Officer Daniel Charles Conroy
- Sergeant John Gerard Coughlin
- Sergeant Patrick T. Coyne
- Detective Christopher Edward Cranston
- Detective Angel Antonio Creagh
- Sergeant Michael Sean Curtin
- Detective Kevin Anthony Czartoryski

- Police Officer John D'Allara
- Police Officer Anthony D'Erasmo
- Detective Annetta G. Daniels
- Police Officer Vincent G. Danz
- Sergeant Garrett S. Danza
- Detective Michael Kenneth Davis
- Police Officer Anthony DeJesus
- Deputy Chief Vincent A. DeMarino
- Police Officer Michael O. Diamond
- Detective Corey J. Diaz
- Detective Leroy Dixon
- Police Officer Kenneth Xavier Domenech
- Police Officer Jerome Mark Patrick Dominguez
- Police Officer Stephen Patrick Driscoll
- Police Officer Renee Dunbar
- Police Officer Robert M. Ehmer
- Police Officer Mark Joseph Ellis
- Police Officer Otto R. Espinoza
- Detective Pedro Esponda, Jr.
- Police Officer William P. Farley
- Police Officer Robert Fazio, Jr.
- Detective Luis G. Fernandez
- Sergeant Paul Michael Ferrara
- Police Officer Keith A. Ferrara
- Police Officer John P. Ferrari
- Police Officer Edward M. Ferraro
- Inspector Donald G. Feser
- Detective Carmen M. Figueroa
- Police Officer Alexander Figueroa
- Police Officer Nicholas G. Finelli
- Detective Stuart F. Fishkin
- Police Officer Edward J. Fitzgerald
- Lieutenant Jeffrey W. Francis
- Sergeant Gary M. Franklin
- Detective Sean Patrick Franklin
- Police Officer Frank L. Gagliano

- Police Officer Scott N. Gaines
- Captain Barry Galfano
- Police Officer Thomas J. Gallagher
- Sergeant Michael J. Galvin
- Police Officer Deborah A. Garbutt-Jeff
- Police Officer Matthew J. Gay
- Police Officer Judy Ann Ghany-Barounis
- Police Officer Anthony C. Giambra, Jr.
- Detective Peter "Pietro" Gianfrancesco
- Detective James Thomas Giery
- Sergeant Rodney C. Gillis
- Captain Edward Charles Gilpin
- Detective Charles Gilbert Gittens, Jr.
- Detective Michael E. Glazer
- Police Officer James Junior Godbee
- Detective John E. Goggin
- Police Officer Michael H. Grannis
- Police Officer Robert C. Grossman
- Police Officer Dave E. Guevara
- Inspector James Guida
- Sergeant Charles R. Gunzelman
- Police Officer Diane F. Halbran
- Police Officer Michael J. Hance
- Police Officer Anthony R. Hanlon
- Sergeant Claire T. Hanrahan
- Police Officer Raymond Harris
- Detective Kevin George Hawkins
- Police Officer Joseph F. Heid
- Police Officer Robert Bernard Helmke
- Detective Michael R. Henry
- Detective Alick W. Herrmann
- Detective William J. Holfester
- Police Officer Richard G. Holland
- Detective Nathaniel Holland, Jr.
- Detective Steven Hom
- Police Officer Demetrias Hopkins

- Detective Charles James Humphry
- Sergeant Michael Vincent Incontrera
- Sergeant Wayne A. Jackson
- Police Officer Richard Jakubowsky
- Police Officer Cheryl D. Johnson
- Police Officer Paul J. Johnson
- Police Officer Louise M. Johnston
- Sergeant Scott Johnston
- Police Officer Robert W. Kaminski
- Police Officer Charles M. Karen
- Detective William D. Kinane
- Police Officer William J. King
- Police Officer Ronald Philip Kloepfer
- Police Officer Gary Lee Koch
- Police Officer Kelly Christine Korchak
- Police Officer Fred J. Krines
- Detective John F. Kristoffersen
- Detective Stephen T. Kubinski
- Police Officer Thomas Michael Langone
- Detective Robert F. Larke
- Sergeant Mark Lawler
- Police Officer James Patrick Leahy
- Detective Michael Lawrence Ledek
- Detective Jeffrey A. Lee
- Inspector Justin C. Lenz
- Police Officer Andrew J. Lewis
- Detective Christian R. Lindsay
- Lieutenant Luis A. Lopez
- Police Officer Richard Lopez
- Detective Thomas J. Lyons
- Police Officer Frank Gerard Macri
- Police Officer David Mahmoud
- Police Officer Shaun M. Mahoney
- Detective John J. Marshall
- Sergeant Robert P. Masci
- Police Officer Vito S. Mauro

- Police Officer Gary Gerald Mausberg
- Lieutenant Jacqueline McCarthy
- Police Officer Brian Grady McDonnell
- Police Officer Patrick Thomas McGovern
- Sergeant Colleen A. McGowan
- Captain Edward Joseph McGreal
- Sergeant Michael J. McHugh
- Police Officer Denis Reid McLarney
- Police Officer Christopher Shawn McMurry
- Lieutenant Jennifer Meehan
- Police Officer Gregory V. Melita
- Detective Tommy L. Merriweather
- Detective Mark Mkwanazi
- Lieutenant Brian S. Mohamed
- Deputy Chief James Gerard Molloy
- Detective James W. Monahan
- Detective Robert A. Montanez
- Detective Michael P. Morales
- Captain Dennis Morales
- Detective John K. Muller
- Sergeant Patrick P. Murphy
- Lieutenant Paul Murphy
- Sergeant Edmund P. Murray
- Sergeant Anthony Napolitano
- Police Officer Mark J. Natale
- Police Officer Robert J. Nicosia
- Detective Maureen M. O'Flaherty
- Sergeant Terrence Scott O'Hara
- Sergeant Donald J. O'Leary, Jr.
- Lieutenant Carlos J. Ocasio
- Police Officer Jason Howard Offner
- Detective Edwin Ortiz
- Police Officer Robert Ortiz
- Police Officer Robert V. Oswain, Jr.
- Police Officer Joseph Cavanaugh Pagnani
- Police Officer Allison Marie Palmer

- Lieutenant Phillip E. Panzarella
- Detective Joseph Paolillo
- Police Officer William G. Parker
- Police Officer Marie Ann Patterson-Bohanan
- Captain Ronald G. Peifer, Sr.
- Police Officer Angelo Peluso, Jr.
- Police Officer John William Perry
- Detective Philip T. Perry
- Police Officer Glen Kerrin Pettit
- Detective Joseph L. Pidoto
- Sergeant Louis R. Pioli
- Captain Peter L. Pischera
- Police Officer Francis Thomas Pitone
- Police Officer Frank J. Pizzo
- Police Officer Nancy A. Puca
- Lieutenant Christopher M. Pupo
- Assistant Chief Michael V. Quinn
- Detective Andrea Renee Jacqueline Rainer
- Police Officer Moira Ann Reddy-Smith
- Police Officer Christine Anne Reilly
- Detective George Clay Remouns, Jr.
- Lieutenant Gerald Rex
- Lieutenant Robert Daniel Rice
- Detective Claude Daniel Richards
- Detective Ronald A. Richards
- Detective Roberto L. Rivera
- Police Officer Lawrence J. Rivera
- Police Officer Peter O. Rodriguez
- Detective Joseph M. Roman
- Lieutenant Kenneth W. Rosello
- Lieutenant John Charles Rowland
- Sergeant Timothy Alan Roy, Sr.
- Lieutenant James D. Russell
- Detective John A. Russo
- Sergeant Michael W. Ryan
- Lieutenant James E. Ryan

- Police Officer Patrice Marie Ryan-Ott
- Detective Thomas Santoro
- Sergeant Stephen P. Scalza
- Sergeant Jacqueline C. Schaefer
- Detective James A. Schiavone, Jr.
- Detective Joseph Edward Seabrook
- Police Officer Peter M. Sheridan, Jr.
- Lieutenant Marci Simms
- Detective Basilio A. Simons
- Detective Andrew L. Siroka
- Sergeant Harold John Smith
- Captain Scott V. Stelmok
- Detective Christopher Strucker
- Police Officer Ramon Suarez
- Sergeant Barbara J. Sullivan
- Police Officer Robert S. Summers
- Detective Traci L. Tack-Czajkowski
- Police Officer Paul Talty
- Police Officer Richard E. Taylor
- Sergeant Edward Doyle "Ned" Thompson
- Detective Sally A. Thompson
- Detective William B. Titus, Jr.
- Police Officer Martin Tom
- Police Officer Reginald Umpthery, Sr.
- Police Officer Santos Valentin, Jr.
- Detective Harry Valentin
- Police Officer Manuel Vargas, Jr.
- Detective Dennis J. Vickery
- Police Officer John F. Vierling, Jr.
- Detective Joseph Vincent Vigiano
- Police Officer Perry T. Villani
- Police Officer Matthew S. von Seydewitz
- Sergeant Michael B. Wagner
- Police Officer William T. Walsh
- Lieutenant William H. Wanser, III
- Detective Thomas P. Ward

- Police Officer Walter Edward Weaver
- Detective Thomas Francis Weiner, Jr.
- Police Officer Ronald Evan Weintraub
- Detective Richard H. Wentz
- Detective Jennifer A. Williams
- Police Officer Wade Jason Williams
- Detective Robert W. Williamson
- Inspector Richard Daniel Winter
- Police Officer Kenneth W. Wolf
- Police Officer George Mon Cheng Wong
- Detective John T. Young
- Detective James Zadroga
- Police Officer Robert A. Zane, Jr.

New York County District Attorney's Office, New York

- Senior Investigator Fred Ghussin

New York State Environmental Conservation Police, New York

- Conservation Officer Stephen Lawrence Raymond

New York State Office of Court Administration, New York

- Senior Court Officer Thomas Jurgens
- Captain William Thompson
- Senior Court Officer Mitchel Scott Wallace

New York State Office of Tax Enforcement – Petroleum, Alcohol and Tobacco Bureau, New York

- Bureau Chief Charles Mills

New York State Office of Tax Enforcement – Revenue Crimes Bureau, New York

- Investigator Clyde Frazier
- Investigator Richard Moore
- Investigator Salvatore Papasso
- Assistant Deputy Commissioner William Pohlmann

New York State Police, New York

- Trooper Michael J. Anson
- Trooper Darryl J. Burroughs, Sr.
- Sergeant Jeffrey M. Cicora
- Trooper Jennifer M. Czarnecki
- Trooper Brian S. Falb
- Investigator Ryan D. Fortini
- Senior Investigator Thomas G. Moran, Jr.
- Trooper Covel Chase Pierce
- Sergeant Charles Robert Salaway
- Investigator Paul R. Stuewer

Newtown Police Department, Connecticut

- Police Officer Stephen A. Ketchum

Paterson Police Department, New Jersey

- Detective Anthony Jospeh Lucanto

Peekskill Police Department, New York

- Detective Charles John Wassil, Jr.

Port Authority of New York and New Jersey Police Department, New York

- Police Officer Christopher Amoroso
- Police Officer Maurice Barry
- Police Officer Charles Barzydlo

- Lieutenant John J. Brant
- Police Officer Liam Callahan
- Lieutenant Robert Cirri
- Police Officer John Mark Cortazzo
- Police Officer Clinton Davis
- Lieutenant William E. Doubraski
- Police Officer Donald Foreman
- Police Officer Gregg Froehner
- Police Officer Thomas Gorman
- Sergeant Lawrence A. Guarnieri
- Police Officer Uhuru Gonja Houston
- Police Officer George Howard
- Police Officer Stephen Huczko, Jr.
- Inspector Anthony Infante
- Detective Thomas M. Inman
- Police Officer Paul Jurgens
- Sergeant Robert Kaulfers
- Police Officer James W. Kennelly
- Police Officer Paul Laszczynski
- Police Officer William James Leahy
- Police Officer David P. LeMagne
- Police Officer John Lennon
- Police Officer John Levi
- Police Officer James Lynch
- Captain Kathy Mazza
- Police Officer Donald McIntyre
- Police Officer Walter McNeil
- Police Officer Mark J. Meier
- Director of Public Safety Fred V. Morrone
- Police Officer Joseph Navas
- Police Officer James Nelson
- Police Officer Alfonse Niedermeyer
- Sergeant Vincent Joseph Oliva
- Police Officer Pavlos D. Pallas
- Police Officer James Parham
- Police Officer Dominick Pezzulo

- Police Officer Bruce Reynolds
- Police Officer Antonio Rodrigues
- Police Officer Richard Rodriguez
- Chief James Romito
- Police Officer John Skala
- Police Officer Walwyn Stuart
- Police Officer Michael Edmund Teel
- Police Officer Kenneth Tietjen
- Police Officer Steven John Tursellino
- Police Officer Nathaniel Webb
- Police Officer Michael Wholey

Suffolk County Police Department, New York

- Police Officer Craig L. Capolino
- Sergeant James Thomas Farrell
- Detective Stephen John Mullen
- Sergeant Dennis Wallace Reichardt

United States Department of Homeland Security – Immigration and Customs Enforcement – Homeland Security Investigations, U.S. Government

- Special Agent Louis Henry Aguirre
- Special Agent Dennis Patrick McCarthy
- Special Agent Edward Joseph Smith
- Special Agent Robert T. Williams
- Special Agent Thomas Michael Wischerth

United States Department of Justice – Bureau of Alcohol, Tobacco, Firearms and Explosives, U.S. Government

- Special Agent William C. Sheldon

United States Department of Justice – Federal Bureau of Investigation, U.S. Government

- Special Agent Dennis Bonelli
- Special Agent Steven A. Carr
- Special Agent William Robert Craig
- Supervisory Special Agent Brian Lawrence Crews
- Special Agent Laurie J. Fournier
- Special Agent Leonard Hatton
- Special Agent Jerry D. Jobe
- Special Agent Mark C. Johnston
- Special Agent in Charge David James LeValley
- Special Agent Mark Joseph Mikulski
- Special Agent Melissa S. Morrow
- Special Agent Robert Martin Roth
- Special Agent Gerard D. Senatore
- Special Agent Rex Aaron Stockham
- Special Agent Paul H. Wilson
- Special Agent Wesley J. Yoo

United States Department of Justice – United States Marshals Service, U.S. Government

- Deputy U.S. Marshal Kenneth J. Doyle
- Deputy U.S. Marshal Betty Ann Pascarella
- Deputy U.S. Marshal Zacarias Toro, Jr.

United States Department of the Interior – Fish and Wildlife Service – Division of Refuge Law Enforcement, U.S. Government

- Refuge Manager Richard Jerry Guadagno

United States Department of the Treasury – United States Secret Service Special Services Division, U.S. Government

- Master Special Officer Craig J. Miller

Yonkers Police Department, New York

- Police Officer Anthony Maggiore
- Lieutenant Roy D. McLaughlin

The Policeman's Prayer to St. Michael

St. Michael, heaven's glorious Commissioner of Police, who once so neatly and successfully cleared God's premises of all its undesirables, look with kindly and professional eyes on your earthly force.

Give us cool heads, stout hearts, hard punches, and uncanny flair for investigation and wise judgment.

Make us the terror of burglars, the friends of children and law-abiding citizens, kind to strangers, polite to bores, strict with law-breakers and impervious to temptations.

In troubles and riots give us sheer muscle without temper; at the police count, give us love for truth and evidence without any thought of self.

You know, St. Michael, from your own experiences with the devil that the policeman's lot on earth is not always a happy one; but your sense of duty that so pleased God, your hard knocks that so surprised the devil, and your angelic self-control give us inspiration.

Make us as loyal to the law of God as we are particular about the law of the land.

And when we lay down our night sticks, enroll us in your heavenly force, where we will be as proud to guard the throne of God as we have been to guard the city of all the people.

I was able to get a photo of the steel beam Cross at Ground Zero.

Afterword

I call them demons, but they are only fleeting memories of what I have actually experienced. I run. I follow. I am followed. Chased. The crisis is upon me, and everything decelerates into slow-motion action. I pull my weapon, my only hope of protection, and in classic Jungian fashion the damn thing jams just when I need to dispatch the beast. I awake, jolted from the nightmare, my heart pounding against my chest as if trying to desperately escape through a locked door.

Nightmares. Daydreams. Fleeting thoughts and flashbacks that make me jump. They lurk, just under the surface, waiting to be triggered by a word or a thought that takes me back to a murky moment. It doesn't help to share it, because no one else comprehends it. No one understands the demons.

Sometimes they were self-inflicted. Sometimes imposed brutally by others. Always, they were a waste, at best—the horrors that humans inflict on themselves, or on their neighbors. The dark side—seen only by its occupants, and those who volunteer to run in headlong to stop the bleeding and destruction. We who tell society—'I'll do this, so you don't have to.'

Our culture knows so little of the reality of life and death any longer. Our organizational memory has run out. Society forgets that which is not glaring at it and demanding its attention like publicity whores on the television every night. Our chicken and beef are presented to us in sterile, uniform Styrofoam trays wrapped in sanitary cellophane and delivered under sparkling lights at the grocery store, blocking the memory that they were only yesterday breathing animals. The true nature of the slaughter and butchery of the living creatures is entirely hidden away from public view—so thoroughly that many of our youth fail to realize that meat comes from live animals. The elderly are shipped off to care centers behind thick curtains and the dead are carted away to mortuaries where they are finally presented in tableau vivant to family and friends just moments before internment in fluffy satin surroundings; the envy of departed Pharaohs.

Those few who elect to work in the dark corners, where the living no longer choose to go; places whose existence the living have lately come to deny. Police. Soldiers. Firefighters. Doctors. Nurses. Sewage workers. Butchers. Morticians. Society asks us to do the dirty work, so they don't have to face the realities of life. Then, many begin to deny those realities, and eventually say really stupid things like, 'We don't need you any longer, because the job you do for us doesn't really produce anything.' So they defund, and foolishly forget those who spared them the reality of the darkness.

I guess that's why it seems so lonely at times. That's why the demons don't fade away. That's why I am so easily pushed over the ledge into the abyss and freefall in the darkness. It's not my imagination. It is my memory. If society defunds me, and those like me who do the dirty work, it will soon become backed up with the sludge of its own sewage. My private nightmare will become our collective reality.

I serve and protect. But I cannot protect you from yourselves. The choice is yours.

Made in the USA
Columbia, SC
30 July 2021